D0290799

The Changing Faces of Economic Insecurity

·THE CHANGING FACES OF ECONOMIC INSECURITY

by JOHN G. TURNBULL

WITH THE ASSISTANCE OF MALCOLM S. COHEN AND MARY PEPPLE

The University of Minnesota Press   MINNEAPOLIS

PUBLISHED IN GREAT BRITAIN, INDIA, AND PAKISTAN BY THE OXFORD
UNIVERSITY PRESS, LONDON, BOMBAY, AND KARACHI, AND IN CANADA
BY THE COPP CLARK PUBLISHING CO. LIMITED, TORONTO

▪ PREFACE

THIS book is an inquiry into man's changing economic destiny as it is being affected, has been affected, and will be affected by the four horsemen of economic insecurity: premature death, old age, unemployment, and accidental injury and sickness. We seek to analyze both the quantitative and qualitative ways in which these forces of insecurity are changing.

This book is also an inquiry into the ways in which society has adjusted to these insecurities: what approaches it has used, what programs it has developed, what problems remain.

The analysis is primarily at the microeconomic level; we deal with individuals and families and their budgets and with their income-maintenance problems, and not with aggregates of transfer payments and their importance for personal income. We are convinced that this latter area — the "macroeconomics" of economic security — is a most important topic and needs investigation,[1] but we have not been able to undertake both tasks here.

Our goal in this study has been to be analytically objective. We hope we have been, though such a position may displease pleaders for special causes, whatever side of the fence they be on. But having made this comment about objectivity, we need to note that we also seek to evaluate social adjustment to economic insecurity. Such evaluation requires a framework of criteria — of value judgments, in effect; these are spelled out in detail at appropriate places in these pages. Though these value judgments are based upon a long study of problems of economic insecurity — and of economic security programing — they do involve many personal choices in the final analysis. For those choices we accept full responsibility.

This study was made possible by a Ford Foundation faculty research

---

[1] Two examples of this approach are J. H. Richardson, *Economic and Financial Aspects of Social Security*, London: Allen and Unwin, 1960, and Richard Titmuss, *Essays on the Welfare State*, New Haven: Yale University Press, 1959.

grant during 1962–63, and these pages were written in 1963–64. Already the picture has altered: the Economic Opportunity Act of 1964 and the Social Security Act Amendments of 1965 (including Medicare) provide but two examples of the changing scene; but a discussion of these and other developments must wait until a later date.

I am indebted to a large number of persons for assistance in this study: Malcolm Cohen did yeoman service in providing research assistance, Mary Pepple in an editorial capacity; Robert J. Myers read the entire manuscript and provided invaluable counsel; Harland Fox, Alfred M. Skolnik, and C. Arthur Williams, Jr., were also of considerable help. I am indebted to all of them.

JOHN G. TURNBULL

■ TABLE OF CONTENTS

List of Tables

List of Illustrations

The Changing Faces of Economic Insecurity

◾ ECONOMIC INSECURITY: ITS NATURE AND SCOPE

A PROFESSOR teaching a class in economic security used to tell his students: "If we were to hold a reunion fifty years from now, about a quarter of you would not be here. You might like to look around and see if you can pick out those who would not be with us. You could, of course, start with me, since my absence is almost a certainty."

This book, too, is about those who will not be with us — about the economic problems caused by their premature departure. But it is also an account of those who *will* be with us, and of their economic problems if they are too old to earn a livelihood. It is also an account of the problems of unemployment, and of the difficulties created by accidental injuries and sickness. Finally, it is an account that seeks to compare these problems as they exist today with the situation half a century ago.

What follows explores certain areas of economic policy, particularly the economic insecurities mentioned above. Specifically, this discussion addresses itself to two major questions: First, has the nature of economic insecurity altered in the past generation? If so, what can be said — quantitatively and qualitatively — about such alterations? And second, changes having occurred, what has been society's response? What kind of accommodation has it made?

The following are examples of the kinds of issues this book is concerned with. First: It has been suggested that a rising price level in the United States after World War II caused a new kind of insecurity through its erosive effect upon the incomes of retired people and others living on fixed incomes. In the public sector, the response to this development was rising benefit levels for various kinds of economic security programs. In the private sector, the variable annuity, designed to permit benefits to adjust more readily to price-level changes, was introduced.

Second, in the past it was held that a person out of work could, with improved economic conditions, probably find a job similar to his old one. Today it is more and more often held that skills go rapidly out of date and that to become re-employable a person may have to be retrained. The responses to this belief have been, on the one hand, private retraining such as that undertaken by Armour and its affiliated unions, and on the other, the public retraining available under the Manpower Development and Training Act and the Area Development Act.

What this book proposes is to examine the changing patterns of economic insecurity and of accommodation to them.

Some Definitions, Assumptions, and Limitations

Security has many faces, related in many complicated ways. I shall focus upon the economic face because that is what I know best.

Economic insecurity may be defined as income curtailment or income insufficiency,[1] and we shall here regard economic security as income maintenance.[2] These terms need, however, to be interpreted in detail and with caution.

One would get little argument about the meaning of insecurity if one defined it as complete cessation of income. Nor would one meet with wide disagreement in defining insecurity as complete cessation of income from employment if that income had been the primary source of support. But suppose a person lives off his income, has $10,000 hoarded in his safety deposit box, and loses his job. Is his a case of insecurity? I should say yes, and divide his problem into two parts: his loss of his job makes him economically insecure, but he has assets that can be used to provide income—that can be used to alleviate the loss of income caused by unemployment.

Concerning income insufficiency: If, for example, his income from a job is not enough for him to live on at a minimum level, a man suffers

---

[1] We are talking here about the *nature* of the concept. If we inquire into the possibilities of the occurrence of insecurity, we get into probability problems, which can be approached quantitatively. If the insecurity is certain, the probability is 1.0, though the risk is 0. The same holds if the probability is 0. Risk is at a maximum where the probability is 0.5. See O. D. Dickerson, *Health Insurance,* Homewood, Ill.: Richard D. Irwin, Inc., 1959, pp. 4–5.

[2] Man has, of course, long searched for security on a broad front — much broader than the income-maintenance front we are using. For one comprehensive account of the worker's quest for security, see the *Monthly Labor Review* for June, 1963, an entire issue devoted to this topic.

from economic insecurity. And if he has additional expenses because of accident or sickness, we should regard this as insufficiency. But we do not regard as insecure people who simply cannot afford a trip around the world. In this sense income is never sufficient — if, that is, one regards man's wants as unlimited.

There are many kinds of borderline case that we could let plague us if we wanted to, but I believe I have now made the concepts clear enough. Insecurity is insufficiency, and insufficiency can occur either on the income side, from an absolute or relative loss of income, or on the outgo side, from an increase in expenses; here I mean only increased expenses resulting from minimum budget demands or because of illness; I exclude problems of keeping up with the Joneses. Poverty, which will be discussed in the last chapter, appears when the insufficiency is extreme or continues for a long time.

Those who are economically insecure because of insufficient income are an overhead cost to society — a cost that cannot be disposed of. The employer can lay off employees if the economy takes a turn for the worse; to him labor is a variable cost. But the resulting unemployed — the economically insecure — are an overhead cost to society; we have no social euthanasia to solve the problem. J. Maurice Clark has stated all this aptly, using labor as an illustration: "In a more general sense, however, there is a minimum of maintenance of the laborer's health and working capacity which must be borne by someone, whether the laborer works or not . . . Thus the burden is there in any case; it cannot be avoided." [3]

A central problem facing all societies is how to meet such overhead, [4] and it has been solved in several ways. Currently in the United States we use a pluralistic approach as to both who and how. Government is assumed to have a major share of responsibility for providing a basic layer of protection (and indeed in some areas it is the only agency capable of doing the job); yet we pay far more than lip service to individual initiative in supplementing this basic layer.

The methods employed have evolved into a highly sophisticated and

[3] *Studies in the Economics of Overhead Costs*, Chicago: University of Chicago Press, 1923, p. 16.

[4] For comments on various economic and philosophical principles involved see Kenneth E. Boulding, *Principles of Economic Policy*, Englewood Cliffs, N.J.: Prentice-Hall, 1958, Ch. 10, and Valdemar Carlson, *Economic Security in the United States*, New York: McGraw-Hill, 1962, Chs. 1, 3, 4, 5.

complex system. Basically, government has explicitly accepted the responsibility for maintaining factor income (here wage and salary income from the labor factor) at minimal levels. This implies a responsibility for maintaining employment at high levels (the Employment Act of 1946) and in higher than substandard conditions (the Fair Labor Standards Act of 1938). These efforts are supplemented by state and local efforts and by employers' and unions' activities.

But such prevention is not always (and empirically cannot always be) successful: some people die prematurely, others inevitably grow old, some people find themselves unemployed, and anyone can incur additional expenses. Thus an alleviation is used to assist those whom prevention has not covered. Such alleviation takes two forms: providing non-factor income or providing supplementary income to meet, perhaps, a medical bill.

The above approaches have altered over the years. Although there are some important exceptions and reversals, explicit income systems have tended to be substituted for implicit service programs.[5] In place of the county old folks' home we have the Social Security check. Again with some important exceptions such as public assistance, economic security program benefits tend to be given as a matter of right rather than on the basis of need.[6] The net effect of these two developments has been to depersonalize the attack upon insecurity. The insurance system and its administrators, public or private, and the economic security check have superseded families and friends not only as the source of assistance but as the means through which it is provided.

Causes of Economic Insecurity

Before we can appraise changes in economic insecurity, we must inquire into the forces which cause it.

We shall attempt to classify causal forces in terms of the kinds of economic security programs society has developed for various sources of insecurity. It immediately becomes apparent that such classification is at the proximate causal level. Unemployment is a causal factor giving

[5] See Eveline M. Burns, *Social Security and Public Policy*, New York: McGraw-Hill, 1956, pp. 5–9.

[6] Some semantic as well as conceptual problems arise out of the use of these terms: a person who demonstrates need may obtain assistance as a matter of right. But this apparent contradiction poses no problem if we are clear about the context in which the terms are applied.

rise to insecurity, but it may well be that one man is unemployed through no fault of his own whereas another cannot find work because he has a reputation as a troublemaker. In short, there are causal forces behind causal forces.

The analysis will usually stop at the proximate level, with some exceptions. Though a full exploration of causality is far beyond my competence, I contend that much that is useful can be said at the proximate level.

All economic insecurity, in our context, can be viewed as income deficiency. Yet in some cases the trigger is falling income, whereas in others the trigger is increased expenses.

The Economic Insecurity of Income Curtailment

On the income curtailment side are the following causes of economic insecurity. Premature death can be regarded as dying too soon. More rigorously, as defined here premature death is dying and leaving behind unfulfilled economic obligations — a wife to be provided for, a mortgage to be paid off, children to be educated. Thus the death of a single person without dependents would not be regarded as premature.

If the breadwinner dies, the drop in income will be accompanied by reduced expenses — one less body to clothe, one less mouth to feed. If the widow has children and has to get a job, the problem is also different. If a wife dies, on the other hand, expenses may increase; a housekeeper may cost more than the wife did.

If premature death is dying too soon, old age is living too long — "too long" standing against the economic backdrop of having outlived one's earning ability. If one could die with his working boots on, old age in this sense would not exist. Whether expenses increase or decrease in old age depends upon individual circumstances. It is likely that medical care will cause an increase, but if the children have been educated and the mortgage paid off, explicit charges may fall, though implicit costs may not.

Here the reader may wonder about the older person who, though he has lost his job, is living comfortably on a pension. The answer is that the pension — and insurance and similar income — is a response to the problem, and will be considered as such.

In premature death and old age the loss of employment is permanent. But in economic unemployment, except for the small number of unemployables (where personal causes are relevant) the loss of employment is presumed to be temporary, caused by deficiencies in aggregate demand or structural changes in the economy. Economic unemployment may go along with increased or reduced expenses: during active job-seeking, expenses may go up; but in the average case expenses change little — decreasing slightly, if anything. If substitute income is provided, as from an unemployment insurance program, one kind of expense, taxes, may fall materially because such income is usually exempt from taxation. Accidental injury and sickness are discussed below as added expenses. But if the victim is the primary breadwinner, the possibility of income curtailment exists: if he cannot work, his pay may well be cut.

The above four categories are the usual examples of economic insecurity caused by a cut in income — an absolute cut in that the actual number of dollars (as contrasted with their value) decreases. But two other factors also operate, though in ways different from those above.

The first is substandard wages — a person is not unemployed, but his wages are below what society finds acceptable. His is an employment contract under socially unacceptable conditions. "Unacceptable" is defined legally and embodied in such statutes as the Fair Labor Standards Act and in wage orders. One may choose to call this curtailment of income "absolute" or "relative," but the variations in terminology do not change the understanding of the problem. The insecurity comes from insufficient income — from the inability to meet a minimum subsistence budget. Too few working hours may also be a cause, though the impact is different.

Price level changes operate in a relative rather than absolute sense, and work through economic security programs as well as through other channels. Two examples can be given, both caused by the erosion of purchasing power because of price increases after World War II. In the first, a man is working but his wages fail to keep up with price increases. Whether his insecurity is acute depends upon the absolute size of his income and the size of the change in prices.

The second person gets his income from the economic security program, but the results are the same. An unemployed worker gets unemployment benefits ; a widow, life insurance payments; a retired person, annuity installments. All (particularly the last two) get fixed amounts, and a price increase leads to relative income loss for all. If the price rise

8

continues over a long period, their problem may become acute: those individuals who retired on a fixed pension in 1945 were markedly worse off by 1955.

The Economic Insecurity of Added Expense

In the "added expenses" category we shall focus here only upon accidental injury and sickness. This choice reflects a choice that society has made: certain kinds of expense are justifiable causes of insecurity; others are not. This choice has both moral and financial bases: to try to get well is morally defensible even if you cannot pay for it; to take a trip around the world or buy a new house may well not be. Getting well involves nondeferrable expenses, but a trip around the world can be deferred forever. We could list justified and unjustified added expenses, and we should all probably agree about the justifiability of spending money to get well. If the accident or sickness befalls the breadwinner, the problem is cruelly compounded, for in addition to the added expense there is an absolute loss of income.

This study deals with income insufficiency and income maintenance. Poverty as a type of income insufficiency will be treated separately in a later chapter; the basic concern will be with interruption of income and its relation to economic insecurity, and with added expense. These are two sides of the same coin, as has been noted: income insufficiency may arise from an income decrease or an expense increase. (And, insofar as price level increases — as noted above — are involved, the dual character of the problem becomes readily apparent.)

Society's Response to Economic Insecurity

The challenge of insecurity has been answered, as we have seen, in many ways: through insurance and noninsurance techniques and by public and private agencies. This is not the place to survey these answers. But, to restate the principal methods of attack: prevent the accident, reduce unemployment, and you likewise prevent or reduce the economic insecurity; it never has a chance to develop if its cause is eliminated or tempered. Though complete prevention is a conceptual possibility, its realization in fact is limited. For those from whom insecurity is exacting its toll — for whom prevention has not worked — some means must be found to alleviate the undesirable economic consequences of insecurity's impact.

It is one thing to talk in general abstract terms about society's response and quite another to clothe the skeleton with the vast detail of current programs. I shall, later and where appropriate, trace with some care the relevant facts about these programs. Here, for two reasons, I shall confine myself to programs providing income as a matter of right rather than need. I believe that income as a matter of right is much better than programs in which need must be exhibited. Need programs require a different kind of analysis, more suitable for the welfare specialist who knows the problems of grinding poverty.

Insecurity Itself

This study seeks to do more than merely describe; it also appraises the changing characteristics of insecurity and the changing responses to it.

Selecting criteria to measure insecurity is relatively simple. The primary one will be reduction, and though this will of necessity be stated in directional terms rather than as specific magnitudes, it should not be difficult to apply. If there is a reduction in mortality or in unemployment or in accidental injury and sickness, the economic insecurity arising therefrom will decrease. We may or may not be able to set goals toward which such reduction ought to proceed. For unemployment we could suggest a realizable ideal — a four per cent maximum. For premature death or accidental injury and sickness, the ideal goal would be zero; but we are uncertain about a realistic goal. Old age is inevitable. Yet we can say something quantitatively useful about the changing incidence of economic insecurity.

Meeting Insecurity

Here the problem becomes more complex and requires a more detailed discussion. We shall apply two kinds of criteria at two different levels: broad ones capable of application to all forms of economic policy; narrower ones particularly suitable to economic security as such.

The general criteria are four originated and developed by Kenneth Boulding: economic progress: the improvement of means; economic stability: the minimization of fluctuations; economic justice: "justice" in distribution; economic freedom: the area of choice within limitations.[7] An ideal accommodation to economic insecurity would meet all

[7] *Op. cit.*, Chs. 1–5.

10

four. An acceptable program would at least not worsen the situation. It is possible, to be sure, for a policy to produce mixed results — to increase progress but to lessen freedom at the same time. Deciding about the acceptability of such policies will await the case-by-case analysis I shall undertake in later chapters.

The specific criteria are as follows: Income maintenance should be based on right rather than need; meaning, for example, that social insurance is more desirable than relief or assistance. Income restoration should be explicit rather than providing implicit services. Where control is needed, the service approach is the more rational; but explicit income affords more freedom of choice. Maximum levels of income compatible with another standard should be restored. The closer the income is to that standard, the more satisfactory the program. Specific standards will be set forth in each of the following chapters. Accommodation to changing costs and prices should be made, though instantaneous adjustment is impossible. If prices rise, the variable annuity permits a better adjustment for the aged than does an annuity providing a fixed income. An economic security program should not destroy incentive. This problem is not likely to arise in premature death or old age, but it may appear in the form of malingering after an accident or illness, and it becomes more serious in economic unemployment. Even though a single system might be the most economical and efficient, a pluralistic system best fits American culture and politics. The government should provide a floor of protection; the thickness of the carpeting on that floor ought to be a matter of individual initiative. How thick the government floor should be for each security program will be discussed later.

Several more criteria will be applied where relevant: where feasible, programs should be jointly financed (that is, contributory); benefits should be related when possible to previous employment or wages; and programs should simultaneously facilitate needed technological change, provide security for the displaced worker, and speed him quickly back to work.

There are various adjustments to economic insecurity, some, in our system of values, preferable to others. The criteria above are a means for selecting the more desirable.

In conclusion: What changes, if any, can be discerned in the pattern of causal forces giving rise to economic insecurity? For such changes as can be discerned, what has been the pattern of social response? This book seeks to answer these questions: What forces cause economic insecurity in my case as they did not for my older brother or sister, my parents, my grandparents? What is being done to combat these insecurities to make this a less burdensome world to live in? How are the weapons different qualitatively and quantitatively from those used in the past?

■ PREMATURE
DEATH

PREMATURE death has been defined (p. 7) as death that leaves financial obligations unmet. A host of exceptions, intriguing conceptually but probably not important quantitatively, might be mentioned. A bachelor businessman — a sole proprietor — may die without heirs, but leaving a business and its employees. Failing to find a new owner, equally competent, the business may wither and the employees lose their jobs. This man's death was not, I think, premature death. A more legitimate exception arises when a person dies without heirs but leaves an accumulation of unpaid bills.

This view of premature death is not, however, operationally acceptable, because statistics are not gathered on this basis. An operationally meaningful measure might distinguish between deaths leaving children, spouse, or parents behind and deaths that do not; but again vital statistics do not record those details.

Ages 14–65 will be considered as the span within which premature death may occur. Before 14, the law limits employment; a youngster would not be likely to be supporting his parents, and this age is a convenient lower limit for marriage. Retirement at 65 is increasingly customary, and employment limited for a different reason. True, retirement at 65 was not common half a century ago, but using this age as a maximum does not do violence to our approach.

Between 14 and 65 death is likely to be premature in our sense; the income problem of premature death is caused by the stoppage of wages and salaries. Before 14 and after 65 a person is less likely to have dependents, and, more than this, before 14 and after 65 he is not likely, or, at the upper range, is less likely, to have wage or salary income interrupted by death.

Frequency

We shall measure premature death as follows: For each age group the probability of living through the year (or dying during the year) can be calculated. If the probability of death for any given year in the age span exhibits a downward drift from a cause, then one may infer that premature death from that cause is a lessening problem.

Matrimony establishes the case of possible prematurity, and changes in the extent of matrimony show its degree. Various combinations of these statistics are possible. Decreasing mortality and fewer families lessen the aggregate problem; increasing mortality and more families heighten it. Decreasing mortality and increasing numbers of families, or vice versa, act as offsets, with the net impact depending upon the degree of each change.

Severity

The two kinds of data above are aggregate: they portray the extent of the problem for the economy as a whole, but they do not reveal its intensity for the surviving dependents. Severity or intensity is a function of several variables — family size and well-being, family finances, and family aspirations. Family size and health are measurable. The larger the family left behind and the poorer their health, the greater the problem. A childless widow has a less serious problem than a widow with half a dozen children. Also measurable are the debt assumed by the family and its assets and hence the ratio of assets to liabilities at the time of death. If debt per family unit has risen over time, relative to income and accumulated assets, then the assumption is that the insecurity has increased. Any other forces which raise or lower the legally unmet economic obligations likewise increase or decrease the problem. Qualitatively important, with quantitative overtones, are the aspirations or expectations of the family relative to income. If today the children of the deceased expect a college education whereas similarly situated children a generation ago did not, the problem is individually more serious than it was earlier.

Mortality Data

Table 1 presents mortality data for men in selected age groups and years. Before we draw conclusions from this table, some precautionary comments must be made. The data are not fully comparable, since they

14

come from several sources. Exact comparability has not been sought because its mathematics would be complicated, and, more important, I believe there is enough inherent variability in the data to preclude exactness — such precision would give only a false sense of exact comparability to the data.

Table 1. Deaths Per 1,000 White Male Population at Specified Ages in Selected Years

				Time of Death				
Age	1843–60*	1900–02	1909–11	1919–21	1929–31	1939–41	1949–51	1961
14	7.60	2.99	2.59	2.58	1.90	1.27	0.90	0.57
20	7.80	5.94	4.89	4.27	3.18	2.12	1.62	1.11
30	8.43	7.99	6.60	5.73	4.13	2.79	1.82	1.42
40	9.79	10.60	10.22	7.50	6.79	5.13	3.91	2.97
50	13.78	15.37	15.53	11.74	12.78	11.55	10.12	7.64
60	26.69	28.59	30.75	24.62	26.44	25.48	23.81	17.27
65	36.87	38.46	40.88	32.39	35.68	34.20	32.07	24.32

* These data are from *American Experience Table* (life insurance company experience, which was predominantly with white males); all other data from *United States Life Tables,* issued (depending upon the year) by United States Department of Commerce, Bureau of the Census or by United States Department of Health, Education, and Welfare, Public Health Service, National Office of Vital Statistics. (Death registration area did not include all states until 1933.)

The pattern of these data is clear: the chance of premature death has decreased for all ages under consideration in the last half century. If one compares the figures for white males for the years 1900–02 with the figures for 1949–51, the following conclusions emerge: At the lower end (age 14) deaths went from 2.99 to 0.90, a decrease of over two thirds (70 per cent): that is, if you were a white male 14-year-old at the turn of the century you had about three chances in a thousand of dying that year; by midcentury the probability would have dropped to one chance in a thousand. Since longevity has tended to increase more markedly at younger ages, one would not expect so great a drop at the upper end, and this is true: a white male age 64 in 1900–02 had 38.46 chances out of 1,000 of dying that year; by 1949–51 the figure was 32.07, a decrease of a sixth (16 per cent).

The probabilities noted above differ not only by age, but also by sex and color.[1] Table 2 and Figure 1 illustrate this and allow us to make a

[1] For details see Mortimer Spiegelman, *Significant Mortality and Morbidity Trends in the United States since 1900*, Philadelphia: American College of Life Underwriters, 1956.

number of observations. At a given time and for a given age group, sex and color groups can be arranged, with some exceptions, in order of increasing mortality as follows:

> White female
> Total population
> White male
> Nonwhite female
> Nonwhite male

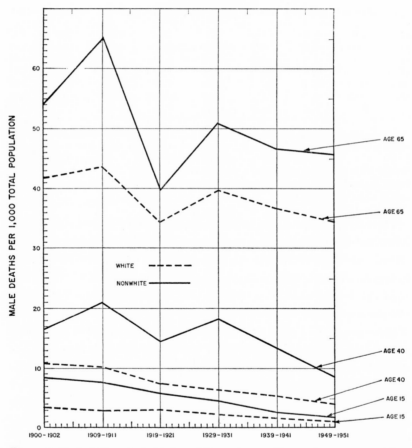

Figure 1. Probability of death for white and nonwhite males, 1900–51. The 1929–31 data show an increase because of the unusually low mortality reported in 1919–21 (supposedly because the flu epidemic of 1918 removed many "weak" lives). The source of these data is *Life Tables for 1949–51*, United States Department of Health, Education, and Welfare, Public Health Service, National Office of Vital Statistics, pp. 26–27.

Table 2. Deaths Per 1,000 Population at Specified Ages in Selected Years *

Age	1909–11 †					1949–51				
	White		Nonwhite		Total Popula-tion	White		Nonwhite		Total Popula-tion
	Male	Female	Male	Female		Male	Female	Male	Female	
15..........	2.83	2.65	7.87	9.49	2.57	1.05	0.53	1.64	1.25	0.87
20..........	4.89	4.20	11.96	10.74	4.68	1.62	0.73	3.14	2.27	1.35
30..........	6.60	6.03	14.96	12.02	6.51	1.82	1.15	4.92	3.90	1.79
40..........	10.22	8.08	21.03	17.50	9.39	3.91	2.42	8.79	7.70	3.68
50..........	15.53	12.59	31.42	25.52	14.37	10.12	5.61	19.09	15.99	8.76
60..........	30.75	25.83	50.79	45.58	28.58	23.81	13.40	36.76	29.54	19.77
65..........	43.79	37.86	64.33	60.87	38.25	34.45	20.63	45.76	37.04	28.43

* *Life Tables for 1949–51*, United States Department of Health, Education, and Welfare, Public Health Service, National Office of Vital Statistics, pp. 26–27.
† Nonwhite means only Negro (who constituted at least 95 per cent of nonwhite population). These data are for death-registration states (ten states and the District of Columbia).

17

This suggests, insofar as the man is the primary breadwinner, that mortality is of a higher frequency and therefore more of a problem than would appear from Table 1 (or from the "Total Population" columns of Table 2). The probabilities are not very different for the white male as compared with the total population, but they diverge appreciably for the nonwhite male.

It is true, however, that the mortality rates even for white males have decreased over the years. The data in Table 2 for 15-year-olds show the following decreases from 1909–11 to 1949–51: nonwhite females (87 per cent), white females (80 per cent), nonwhite males (79 per cent), white males (63 per cent); for the 65-year-olds, white females (46 per cent), nonwhite females (39 per cent), nonwhite males (29 per cent), white males (21 per cent). These kinds of terminal-year comparisons should be viewed with caution, but they suggest an order of magnitude that is illustrative. Oddly enough, white males, the largest group for whom premature death is a problem, have had the smallest decrease.

A lessening of the problem is brought about because mortality tends to be lower among the married than among those "who remain single or those whose marriage has been broken by death or divorce. The married have an advantage at every period of life, particularly prior to age 45, when most families have young children in their care. Thus, among males aged 20–44, the death rate for the married is only about half that for the single and an even smaller fraction of that for the widowed or divorced. The differentials are not as large among females." [2]

In the nature of things, mortality appears to be approaching an irreducible minimum. Cures for degenerative disease may still cause marked reductions among the elderly. But at all ages the rate of decrease has slowed down, as estimates made in 1957 by T. N. E. Greville for the Division of the Actuary of the Social Security Administration show and as several examples from the projected annual mortality rates (per 1,000) for the year 2000 illustrate: For United States males age 20 in 1939–41 the mortality rate was 2.46; in 1949–51 1.79; for 2000, low mortality projections are 1.22, high 1.76. For United States males age 60 the respective figures are 26.47, 24.82, 12.60, and 21.12. The midpoint between low and high projections is 1.49 for the 20-year-old, 16.86 for the 60-year-old.[3]

[2] *Statistical Bulletin*, Metropolitan Life Insurance Company, February, 1957.
[3] *Illustrative United States Population Projections*, United States Department of

Measuring Frequency: Family Formation

Tables 3 and 4, presenting selected data about family formation, allow us to draw some conclusions. The percentage of married people in the total population age 14–64 has risen over the years, a sizable part of the increase taking place from 1940 to 1950. Furthermore, there is

Table 3. Data on Numbers of Married (in thousands) for Selected
Years, by Age Group

| | | Age 14–64 | | |
Year	No. of Married Couples 65 and Over *	Total Population	Married Couples	Married People†
1910	16,409	56,572	29.14%	58.28%
1960	35,530	104,264	35.04	70.08
1980 (est.) ..	50,900	147,200	34.50	69.00

Sources: *Thirteenth Census of the United States, 1910*; *Current Population Reports*, United States Department of Commerce, Bureau of the Census (Series P-25, No. 187); and *United States Census of Population, 1960*.

* Adjusted for population age, though this is subject to some error, since it is difficult to adjust the data when one spouse is over 65, the other under.

† Robert J. Myers points out that only this column affords a basis for valid comparison. He notes that it does not seem reasonable to compare married couples with total population.

reason to believe (failing a major reversal such as that in the early 1920's or the mid-1940's) that the percentage of married people has reached its peak and will henceforth remain stationary or move downward, though it might swing temporarily upward in the near future as the record crop of war babies reaches marrying age. The marriage rate per 1,000 inhabitants in the early 1900's was 10.1; in 1960 it was 8.5.[4] For the same period, the rates per 1,000 females aged 15–44 were 42.8 and 42.3 respectively. The divorce rate per 1,000 inhabitants has increased from 0.8 to 2.2; that per 100 marriages from 8 to 26, all these between the early 1900's and 1960.

The increase in the number of married couples in 1960 relative to the population aged 14–64 has been on the order of 20 per cent. The projec-

Health, Education, and Welfare, Social Security Administration, Division of the Actuary (Actuarial Study No. 46), 1957, p. 14; this analysis does show a marked reduction in older age mortality.

[4] The use of aggregate crude rate for marriage, death, and birth is fraught with danger because of changing age distribution. The 1910 rate was higher than the 1960 because in 1960 there were far more people under age 15 and over age 65.

Table 4. Married Couples (in thousands) in Relation to Total Population for Selected Years, Including Projections *

Year	No. of Married Couples	Total Population	Married Couples in Total Population
1910.........	17,175	92,407	18.59%
1930.........	25,174	123,188	20.44
1940.........	28,517	132,122	21.58
1950.........	35,006	151,683	23.08
1960.........	40,205	180,670	22.25
1965†........	42,989	198,950	21.61
1970†........	46,720	219,474	21.29
1975†........	51,239	243,880	21.01
1980†........	56,216	272,557	20.63

Sources: *Thirteenth Census of the United States, 1910; Current Population Reports,* United States Department of Commerce, Bureau of the Census (Series P-25, No. 187); and *United States Census of Population,* 1930, 1940, 1950, 1960.

*As Robert J. Myers points out (see note to Table 3), there are difficulties in comparing married couples with total population.

† Series A (one of several alternative projections).

tions of Tables 3 and 4 suggest not a further increase, but a decrease. Hence the following conclusions appear warranted.

Mortality and Matrimony

Falling mortality decreases the frequency of premature death; rising matrimony increases its likelihood. One may conclude that for all ages in our 14–64 groups the decrease in mortality over the last half century has been greater than the increase in matrimony.

An ideal quantitative method of appraising the twin impacts of mortality and matrimony would be to compare the percentage changes in each of them for each age group for the time period, but this is difficult. A convenient alternative is to assume that the increase in marriages (i.e., the change in marital status) applies evenly to all ages in the 14–64 group and then to compare this with the changes in mortality rate at various ages.

We assume that the increase in married couples adjusted for population increases over the past half century has been on the order of 20 per cent for the age brackets in which we are interested (though the proportion married by age has risen much more at the younger ages than at the middle and older ages). In three cases selected for illustrative purposes,

20

mortality for the same period decreased over 80 per cent for the 14-year-old, over 70 per cent for the 40-year-old, and over 35 per cent for the 64-year-old; the degree of improvement is clear.

We may therefore conclude that in terms of relative frequency premature death as a cause of economic insecurity is not so serious a problem as it was half a century ago.

Measuring Severity: Family Size

For any given number of married couples, the more children per couple, the more severe the problem created by premature death. The accompanying tabulation shows the number of children under 22 per married couple in 1790, 1910, 1940, and 1960;[5] precision is difficult if not

1790	+3.0
1910	2.4
1940	1.6
1960	1.8

impossible in these calculations, but general trends are discernible. These data suggest a long, slow decrease in the number of children per family, reaching a low point around 1940, after which the number rose again.[6] Census data illustrate this in a slightly different way. The average population under 18 per family in 1940 was 1.24, in 1950 1.17, in 1961 1.44.[7] Current fertility and mortality trends suggest no reversal of the recent increase in the number of children per family, but neither do they lead one to infer that a return to the more than three children per married couple of the 1790's is likely.[8]

One aspect of these changes deserves further brief comment. The families of younger husbands — up to 35 — have shown the most marked increases recently: between 1940 and 1958 such families increased 44.2

[5] Adapted from P. C. Glick, "Family Trends in the United States 1890–1940," *American Sociological Review*, August, 1942, and from *Current Population Reports,* United States Department of Commerce, Bureau of the Census (Series P-20).

[6] Children under 5 per 1,000 women 20–44 were 1,281 in 1800, 609 in 1910, 400 in 1940, and 551 in 1950. See Wilson H. Grabill, Clyde V. Kiser, and Pascal K. Whelpton, *The Fertility of American Women,* New York: John Wiley, 1958, Table 7.

[7] "Household and Family Characteristics," *Current Population Reports,* United States Department of Commerce, Bureau of the Census (Series P-20, No. 116), March, 1961. Since a family is a broader concept than a married couple, one would expect to find, for the same number of children, fewer per family than per married couple.

[8] A different way of looking at this is as percentage distribution among age groups. In 1900 dependent children (under 15) made up 34.4 per cent of the population; in 1940 25.0 per cent; in 1955 29.6 per cent. See Conrad Taeuber and Irene B. Taeuber, *The Changing Population of the United States,* New York: John Wiley, 1958, p. 31.

per cent in children under 18, whereas families of husbands 45–54 decreased 12.9 per cent. This could make the problem of premature death more serious; the younger father is more likely to have younger children and less likely to have established himself.[9] Projections to 1975 suggest that marriages with husbands 14–24 will show the greatest relative increase. The severity of the problem of premature death may therefore also be expected to become greater in the same period.[10]

Detailed data are not available about the physical condition of wives and children left behind by the premature death of the breadwinner, and it is hard to measure physical well-being anyhow. But progress in medicine, in safety programs, and in nutrition have made today's children healthier than yesterday's; the survivors should therefore be better off today than a half century ago.

Children per married couple decreased for a long time, concomitantly lessening the problem of premature death, until the 1940's when a reversal took place. The increase has been modest, however, and there is no prospect of a marked increase in the problem's future severity. But child labor was commoner in 1910 than in 1960, and yesterday's children less dependent upon their parents than today's; in this sense, premature death is now more of a problem. Men are becoming fathers younger and having more children younger. Since the young man is likely to have less money, this compounds the problem, and this aspect of the problem is likely to become more severe during the next several decades. Today's children are healthier than those a generation ago, lessening the need to supply medical care to the ailing child left behind by a prematurely dead father. This part of the problem is less serious than a generation or two ago, though medical care itself is more costly now. Balancing these facts, we can conclude that the problem is less severe than it was fifty years ago, though the improvement cannot be measured precisely.

Returning to frequency and linking it to severity, we have set them forth in Table 5, which shows the chances of death in typical families. The young father is less likely to be the first member of the family to die. In well-established families it is likely that the husband will die be-

---

[9] To be sure, mortality is less likely for the younger father. In the aggregate, the lower frequency therefore offsets the higher severity, but for those who do die the problem is more serious.

[10] For data see *Current Population Reports*, United States Department of Commerce, Bureau of the Census (Series P-20, No. 90).

Table 5. Chance That Husband Will Die within Specified Number of Years and Corresponding Chances of at Least One Death among Members of a White Family in the United States in 1954*

| Age of Members in Typical Families | | | | | Chances Per 1,000 of Dying | | | | | | | | | | | |
Hus-band	Wife	Children 1st	2nd	3rd	Within 5 Years Hus-band	Oth-ers	Total	Within 10 Years Hus-band	Oth-ers	Total	Within 15 Years Hus-band	Oth-ers	Total	Within 20 Years Hus-band	Oth-ers	Total
20	19	1			9	8	17	17	14	30	26	21	46	38	33	70
25	23	3	1		8	11	19	17	20	36	30	32	61	50	52	99
30	28	6	3	1	9	14	23	22	28	49	42	48	88	76	78	149
35	32	9	6	4	13	13	26	33	31	63	68	59	122	120	97	205
37	34	11	8	4	15	15	30	41	36	75	82	67	144	142	109	235
39	36	13	10	6	19	17	35	50	42	90	99	77	169	168	123	271
41	38	14	10	6	23	19	41	61	47	105	118	86	194	199	136	307
43	40	15	11	7	29	21	49	74	53	123	140	97	223	233	152	349
45	41	16	12	8	35	23	58	89	57	142	166	103	252	272	162	390

Source: *Statistical Bulletin*, June, 1957, Metropolitan Life Insurance Company.
* Mortality based on United States life tables for 1954.

fore any other member of the family. For husbands 35 or older, the chances of death within ten years are greater than for the rest of the family; for husbands 40 and older, the chance is greater within one year.

Family Debt and Net Worth

The greater the unpaid debt left behind the severer the problem for the survivors. If the debt is for goods that can be attached and returned or sold, the problem may not be so serious as where the debt is for items already fully consumed, though whereas repossession of a second car may pose few problems, repossession of furniture is a great hardship.

Over the past half century in the United States, with rising productivity and increasing wealth, we should expect members of society to be better off. This appears to have been true, though relative to levels of aspiration it is not clear how great the quantitative improvement has been. The distribution of income and wealth has not been uniform and a poverty fringe exists for whom the problem is still perhaps as serious as it formerly was.[11]

Table 6 illustrates these trends. The data on this table for years before 1957 are not comparable with the data for 1957 and after because in 1957 corporate securities were included for the first time. More useful comparisons can be made among years between 1929 and 1956 and for years from 1957 to 1960. Moreover, the data are in current dollars — not adjusted for price changes.

This price change problem involves the prices of assets themselves (and changes in those prices over time) and changes in the prices of the goods and services which the assets, if liquidated, could command. With respect to the first no correction need be applied, because it is the value of the assets in the year in question that is important: if the price of a security doubles from Year 1 to Year 2, we are interested only in its price in Year 2: if it has to be liquidated in Year 2 to meet the obligations resulting from premature death, we want to know how many dollars it will provide at that time. (In a different context we might, of course, be interested in knowing how much of the dollar value of assets came from saving and how much from capital appreciation or depreciation. But that is not the case here.)

---

[11] For comments on and an analysis of this kind of problem see Boulding, *op. cit.*, Ch. 10, and James N. Morgan, Martin H. David, Wilbur J. Cohen, and Harvey E. Brazer, *Income and Welfare in the United States*, New York: McGraw-Hill, 1962, Ch. 1.

Table 6. Assets and Liabilities of Individuals in the United States at Ends of Selected
Years, 1929–60, in Billions of Current Dollars

	1929	1933	1939	1945	1950	1955	1956	1957	1958	1959	1960
Assets											
Currency and bank deposits	37.5	30.8	45.1	117.2	130.7	159.0	163.5	163.6	173.9	177.4	181.3
Savings and loan associations ...	6.2	4.8	4.1	7.4	13.9	21.9	37.0	45.0	51.5	58.8	66.8
Insurance and pension reserves...	17.3	19.2	33.0	69.4	108.0	160.0	171.1	184.0	195.5	207.3	219.7
Securities (noncorporate)	14.1	16.3	17.0	70.4	80.0	84.9	88.8	95.0	92.0	101.0	102.1
Corporate and other securities...							335.0*	268.6	360.6	405.0	389.1
Total †	75.1	71.0	99.2	264.4	332.6	435.8	460.4	756.2	873.6	949.4	959.1
Liabilities											
Mortgage debt	12.3	10.0	11.5	13.1	37.6	79.2	89.7	98.4	108.1	121.5	132.4
Consumer debt	5.4	2.4	5.6	3.9	17.9	33.9	37.0	40.2	40.5	46.5	50.2
Securities, loans ‡								4.2	4.6	4.8	5.0
Total	17.7	12.4	17.1	17.0	55.5	113.1	126.7	142.7	153.2	172.8	187.6
Total individuals' net equity.....	57.4	58.6	82.1	247.4	277.2	322.7	333.7	613.5	720.4	776.6	771.5

Source: *The Economic Almanac, 1958*, p. 380; *1962*, p. 409, National Industrial Conference Board.
* Not given in source; estimated figure.
† Totals for some years affected by rounding.
‡ Not given in source for 1929, 1933, 1939, 1945, 1950, 1955, and 1956.

Therefore the analysis adjusts only for changes in the prices of things bought. To do this, the Consumers' Price Index is used and applied to the absolute figures of net equity in Table 7 for the paired years 1929 and 1956, 1957 and 1960.[12] We shall also divide the net equity (as deflated) by total population for the years in question, providing per-capita net equity. Table 7 presents this material.

Table 7. Net Equity and Per-Capita Equity in Selected Years

Year	Value of the Dollar *	Population (millions)	Unadjusted (billions)	Net Equity Adjusted Total (billions)	Net Equity Adjusted Per Capita
1929	136.4	121.8	$ 57.4	$ 78.3	$ 643
1956	86.1	168.2	333.7	287.3	1,708
1957	83.2	171.2	613.5	510.4	2,981
1960	79.1	180.7	771.5	610.3	3,377

* 1947–49 = 100.

This table shows that per-capita net equity has risen over the years, approximating $3,400 in 1960. Though the stock market decline of May, 1962, lowered this figure, recovery was effected by 1963 and new levels reached by 1964. In spite of short-run deviations, the long-run trend is growth. This increase means that the ability to command goods and services out of assets has increased in the last quarter century. Debt has risen over the years; it has been more than counterbalanced by increased assets. The severity of premature death has become less serious in this respect.[13]

Levels of Aspiration

Assuming that the net equity left behind by one prematurely dead is much higher in buying power now than it was a generation ago, the children left behind have aspirations the deceased did not have — the desire for a college education, for example. At the current cost of ful-

[12] We do not use comparative percentage changes here because it would be misleading to do so since the size of the absolute bases from which one works varies. Assume that in Year 1 one has assets of 100, liabilities of 10, and a net equity of 90. In Year 2, assets increase 50 per cent to 150, but liabilities 100 per cent to 20: the percentage increase of the liabilities is double that of the assets, but one is clearly better off in Year 2, for one has a net equity of 130 by contrast with 90 in Year 1.

[13] Again nothing is said at this point about the way such net equity is distributed among the population. This issue will be discussed later in this chapter and in the last chapter.

filling such a desire, we can say several things about the relation of aspirations to the severity of the impact of premature death. The wife and
children may hope that they will not need markedly to lower their level
of living, and the children will want certain advantages that their parents did not have. It is difficult to quantify these desires and the
changes they cause, and it is just as troublesome to ascertain the degree
to which expectations and aspirations press upon income. We can only
conjecture as follows.

Families more and more hope and expect that the premature death of
the breadwinner will not cause a complete change in their pattern and
level of living. Today a married couple usually sets up on its own rather
than living with parents, and if this family should be disrupted by premature death, the survivors now seek to maintain their own entity as
a family instead of moving back with one set of parents. The severity
of the problem has increased as a result: in place of the unused resources
(extra space) that may exist in the home of one set of parents, new
resources must be created to allow the younger family to keep its inde-
pendence.

How much this costs is hard to say; it must cover separate living
quarters, and baby-sitting costs, should the widow go back to work.
Food and clothing need cost no more, however. One might suggest that
it requires a capital sum necessary to provide sufficient income (the
capital plus earnings thereon) to meet the costs of separate quarters
plus other care. At three to four per cent a sum of twenty to thirty
thousand dollars might be required.

Though many factors affect children's aspirations, one thing is sure:
they have increased.[14] At a temporary low in 1934, 66.9 per 1,000 of
the population 18–24 were in institutions of higher learning; by 1958
the number was 231.2. In 1930, 29 per cent of the population 17 years
old graduated from high school; by 1958 64.8 per cent. In 1900, 27,300
degrees of all kinds were granted, in 1959 467,000, and one projection for
1970 is 866,000.[15] More money might be regarded as necessary for more
education, but increased desires are also important. In this area the
severity problem may be more serious than it was. One might argue

[14] For examples of factors influencing educational aspiration, see Morgan, *et al., op. cit.*,
Parts V, VI.
[15] All the data in this paragraph are from *Health, Education, and Welfare Trends, 1960
Edition*, United States Department of Health, Education, and Welfare, pp. 56–63.

that the quantitative degree of severity is the increased cost of education less whatever can be earned by the student. And, if one heeds the advice of vocational counselors that the best defense against unemployment is education and their suggestion that education is an important growth determinant, the problem will increase in intensity.[16]

A Balance Sheet

Proportional increases in the number of married couples have caused premature death to be increasingly severe, though this increase has almost worked itself out and, except for short-run fluctuations, long-run changes are not likely to be for the worse. While liabilities have increased over time, so have assets, and today's family is better off than the family of a half or a quarter century ago. Levels of expectation and aspiration have risen, heightening the problem. Increases in real productivity may have been most important, and severity on balance is therefore less of a problem today than previously.

Yesterday and Today

Where does one stand, then, in comparison with his parents or grandparents in the matter of the incidence and intensity of premature death?

His chances of dying prematurely are fewer. If he was 40, the chances of death in 1960 were fewer than four out of a thousand; his father, 40 in 1930, would have faced seven chances out of a thousand of dying; his grandfather, 40 in 1900, would have stood a little better than nine chances. Of course, these rates would vary depending upon circumstances: for the nonwhite they would be higher, for a white female lower, and for the married lower.

He would be more likely to be married than members of both his father's and his grandfather's generation, but he would also stand a greater chance of being divorced. His grandson may have about the same chance of being married as he does, but his grandson's chance of divorce will be higher.

The number of children in his family would be more than in his father's family, but fewer than in his grandfather's. Very roughly speaking, he would have two children, compared with one and a half for his

[16] See Edward F. Denison, *The Sources of Economic Growth in the United States and the Alternatives before Us*, New York: Committee for Economic Development, 1962, Chs. 7, 21, and Part IV.

father, and nearly three for his grandfather. Since fertility assumptions vary widely, the size of his grandson's family is conjectural; my estimate is that it will be smaller than his.

He would be better off in real terms (assets) than his father or his grandfather. His individual average net worth would be about $3,400, compared with his father's $640 and his grandfather's less than half of that.[17] The expected rate of growth should put his grandson in a relatively better position than his.

The expectations and aspirations of his family would be higher than for either of his forebears. If he should die, his family would be more likely than were the families of his mother or grandmother to wish to continue to live as they have, and not to move in with the grandparents. Educationally, his children appear to have a greater desire to go to college than did their predecessors. As a realistic postscript: I have three children, all of whom would like to go to college; two of my three brothers and sisters went to college; but neither my father nor my mother nor any of their brothers and sisters, some fifteen in all, did; only one went to high school. My grandchildren will have higher aspirations than their parents. Opportunity, of course, plays a role in achieving one's aspiration.

The Preventive Ideal and Current Reality

The ideal approach to the insecurities created by premature death is through the completely effective preventive route: permit no one with unmet economic obligations to die. In our age–marital obligation framework, this means a moratorium on deaths for married primary breadwinners 14 to 64. Prevention has not been unsuccessful, though success should be measured in terms of reduction rather than of one hundred per cent prevention. The figures in the United States Life Tables for successive decades attest to this reduction, but it is not reasonable to expect prevention to be wholly successful, on two grounds. First, man is heir to many ills it is unlikely that medical science will entirely eradicate, and even if he were rid of these internal demons, outside forces are always capable of producing premature death as long as automobiles run, lightning flashes, and ships sail. "Death, as the Psalmist saith, is certain to all; all shall die."

[17] These are averages. Throughout this study when I use (or imply) the word average I define it as the mean, not the median or mode.

Therefore, while prevention continues vitally important, the greater its success, the more difficult further improvement becomes. How close we are to the irreducible minimum is a matter of conjecture, but it is safe to say that we are not so close as to preclude need for the alleviative approach to which we now turn.

The Alleviative Ideal and Current Reality

The ideal protection against premature death would be income sufficient to permit the family to live on in the same way. This income would be lower than before, since there would be one less person's needs to be met.

Such an income must come from somewhere. One way to arrange for it is through public taxation: taxes are collected from those not victims of premature death and paid to the families of those who are. Certain of our public programs (such as the assistances) operate in this manner. A more common way is by creating a capital sum which, either through its interest or through interest plus using the capital, provides the income. A capital sum need not be regarded as sacred; it could be used so as to be reduced to zero when it is no longer needed — as when the children are grown and the widow has died. If the capital sum is itself used, the amount required to provide a given income is obviously less than if it is not.

Other less rigorous income ideals range from a minimum budget to half: "a surviving family, it has been estimated, can live three-quarters as well on half its former income." [18] C. Arthur Williams, Jr., suggests that while "no specific yardstick has been suggested for survivor groups," one might be developed through suitably adjusting the urban worker's "modest but adequate" budget developed by the United States Department of Labor. [19] We shall hereafter refer to this budget and its family as the USDL family.

This budget, compiled for an urban worker 38, his wife 36, a son 13, and a daughter 8 living in a rented dwelling, was costed out for a number of American cities. In 1960, the budgets averaged out between some $5,400 and $6,600. If we choose the single figure $6,200, we shall have

[18] See *Decade of Decision*, New York: Institute of Life Insurance in cooperation with Health Insurance Institute, 1961, p. 13.

[19] J. G. Turnbull, C. Arthur Williams, Jr., and E. F. Cheit, *Economic and Social Security*, New York: Ronald Press, 1962, p. 53.

to adjust it downward to eliminate the expenses of the deceased father. After careful appraisal we might reach $4,500 as a justifiable figure, assuming that the cost of certain overhead such as housing might not change very much, whereas food and clothing would, and that taxes and insurance would decrease more than proportionately; we should then be left with less than three fourths of the $6,200.

This $4,500 we shall call a nondeferrable expense budget throughout. Nondeferrable expenses, those that cannot be put off, vary between the short and long run. Were our family to need help for only a month out of a year, this budget could be less than half of $4,500. But we are talking about long periods — the time until the children are 18.

To provide an income of $4,500 to meet this nondeferrable expense budget one would, if he wanted his capital sum intact at the end of the payout period, need $150,000 if the interest rate were 3 per cent, $112,-500 if it were 4 per cent. But there is no reason to regard capital as sacred, as I have said. How much less would be required if the capital were spent depends upon our assumptions about the period for which benefits are to be paid for the children and when the widow's "life benefit" is to begin. If we used the city-worker budget assumptions, and provided for the children until 18, one child would require income for five years, the other for ten. If we assume $100 a month for each child, this means the $4,500 a year for five years, then $3,300 for another five years, and then $2,100 for the remainder of the widow's life. At her death nothing would be left.

The amount required in this case would vary, depending upon the assumptions one made about the lump sum desired at death and the payout tables currently used by insurance companies. In our calculations we estimated that approximately $67,000 would be required; such a figure underestimates the magnitude of the problem for families whose children are more numerous than two or younger than 13 and 8.

The Social Security Administration uses a different set of family circumstances for illustrative purposes. Though these purposes are not budgetary (they are designed to highlight OASDI benefit payments), they afford a convenient alternative. A father 30 dies leaving a wife 25 and two children 3 and 1.[20] The sum required would be approximately $87,000. Hereafter we shall refer to this family as the OASDI family.

[20] See Bertram Oppal, *Estimated Amount of Life Insurance in Force as Survivor Benefits under OASDI, 1959–60,* United States Department of Health, Education, and Wel-

Extremes could be cited: a childless couple where the wife is close to 65, or the couple with half a dozen children under 10 and a wife under 30. But our OASDI and USDL families provide a useful and realistic basis for illustration, examination, and comparison.

Although there is no unanimity on how much of these budgets should be provided by government programs as a floor of protection, one may suggest that while the children are under 18, two thirds of the income should be afforded by government programs, and thereafter, until the widow remarries or otherwise changes her status, the government should provide half the budget, assuming, of course, that she cannot get a job.

Taking $67,000 (USDL family) or $87,000 (OASDI family) as alleviative ideals because these capital sums would provide modest but adequate budgets for these families, we can find out how close today's families, as well as yesterday's, come to this ideal.

Table 8 represents a first step; it assumes that all assets are evenly distributed among the relevant population, and for 1960 first that all insurance is on the life of the primary breadwinner and then, more realistically, that insurance is prorated on the lives of other than the primary breadwinner. The 1910 figure is a single figure only.

Our budget for 1960 was $4,500. Using data for 1910–15 and adjusting for size of family we arrive at $725 as a reasonable estimate for that period; [21] the improvement in the past fifty years is evident from these data.[22] In 1910, it would have taken $18,125 at 4 per cent to provide the $725 or $24,166 at 3 per cent, assuming the capital were to remain intact. If, instead, the principal could be used, the amounts required would be approximately $11,500 (USDL family) and $14,500 (OASDI family).

In 1910, the protection required by the USDL family was $11,500, compared with protection available of $1,200 — about 10 per cent. The OASDI family would have required $14,500, compared with the $1,200

fare, Social Security Administration, Division of the Actuary (Actuarial Study No. 54), 1961, p. 4.

[21] Details of these budgets are found in Table 20; the chapter gives both premature death and old age budget calculations.

[22] That there has been a real upgrading of the budget over time is clear. We carried the $4,500 budget to 1910 by adjusting for changes in prices only; the result was $1,450. The fact that the budget existing at the time was $725 indicates that the family budget has been upgraded 100 per cent in its components in the half century.

Table 8. Capital Sums Per Family in the United States in 1910 and 1960

Year	No. of Married Couples * (thousands)	Total Life Insurance in Force † (hundreds of thousands)	Life Insurance Per Married Couple	Total Social Security Insurance in Force ‡ (hundreds of thousands)	Social Security Per Married Couple	Net Equity Per Married Couple §	Total Capital Sum
1910	16,409	$ 14,908	$ 909	....	....	$ 300 (est.)	$ 1,209
1960 ‖	36,530	586,448	16,054	$571,000	$15,631	4,300	35,985
1960 ¶	36,530	469,159	12,843	528,000	14,454	4,300	31,597

* From Table 3.
† *Life Insurance Fact Book, 1962*, Institute of Life Insurance, p. 12.
‡ Bertram Oppal, *Estimated Amount of Life Insurance in Force as Survivor Benefits under OASDI, 1959–60*, United States Department of Health, Education, and Welfare, Social Security Administration, Division of the Actuary (Actuarial Study No. 54, 1961), p. 19.
§ From Table 7, adjusted for insurance reserves. Note that this averages out to approximately $2,150 per capita. If the married couple has two children, the sum should double, becoming $8,600.
‖ Assumes all insurance in force on life of primary breadwinner.
¶ Insurance prorated for that on lives of other than primary breadwinner.

available, or approximately 8 per cent. In 1960 the USDL family needed protection of $67,000 and had available $31,600, 47 per cent, whereas the OASDI family needed $87,000 and also had available $31,600, or 36 per cent.

But this approach and these figures understate the protection currently available because of a distributional factor in private insurance and because of protection on the basis of family size rather than face amount in OASDI. Let us look at each of these in turn.

If the life insurance in force in 1960 were distributed evenly among married couples, the average amount per couple would be $12,843.[23] But the average is higher when it is needed most, during the years when the family is growing and growing up, and less later when it is less needed. The first reason for this is that from 14 to 21 less protection is bought, and, conversely, as people get older the amount of insurance they carry tapers off, as when, for example, term-insurance policies are dropped. And secondly, on the cost rather than the protection side, family-income policies, providing additional protection through temporary term insurance, are concentrated in families where the need exists. There is a bunching of protection, for which the unit costs are less. For example, you are an older person with $8,562 of face value in policies; I, with a family, have $17,124 in a family-income plan. The average is $12,843, but this misrepresents the dispersion of protection as well as its cost. The $12,843 average ought perhaps to be adjusted: lowered for the younger and the older and increased in the 20–50 bracket. One set of estimates shows that the amount of the average policy held by men 15–19 is $5,850, by men 55 and over $7,880, but by men 40–44 $14,240;[24] the degree of protection is higher where needed than the $12,843 suggests.

The understatement because of the OASDI program is a more complex problem. The level of private insurance in force depends directly upon protection available and upon the well-being of those affected by premature death. Protection is related to insurance carried. But insurance in force is not an accurate measure of protection available under OASDI, which does not depend upon the face value of policies owned,

---

[23] We continue to assume here that it is evenly distributed among the population, i.e., that the wealthy do not have more in force and the poor less. The evidence strongly suggests, however, that the median would be lower than the mean amount of protection; hence we no doubt overstate our case in this analysis.

[24] *Life Insurance Buying, 1960*, New York: Institute of Life Insurance, 1961, p. 7.

but on family size. As of 1960, a widow under 62 and two children (under 18, or older if disabled) could receive as much as $254 a month (or $3,048 annually) plus a $255 (lump-sum) death benefit. Payments of this size would be available to those whose average yearly earnings after 1950 were $4,000 or more. For $3,600 average annual earnings the monthly payments would be $236.40; the death benefit $255. For average yearly earnings of $800 or less, the monthly payments would be $60 (the minimum), the death benefit $120.

If we took average gross weekly earnings in manufacturing in 1955 ($75.70) and multiplied this figure by 50 to get annual earnings, we would obtain (rounded) $3,800.[25] Under the current benefit plan, these earnings would yield $254 a month,[26] or (rounded) $3,000 a year, as well as a $255 lump-sum death benefit.

If $4,500 is a desirable minimum for the sample surviving family, OASDI protection currently provides $3,000 a year of it for a widow under 62 with two children under 18 (here it makes no difference whether we use as an example the USDL or the OASDI family), leaving $1,500 to be provided by other means.

The USDL family widow is 46 when her youngest child becomes 18, and for the next sixteen years (until she is 62) she has no OASDI income; the OASDI family widow has no OASDI income from 42 to 62. After she reaches 62, the widow could collect $90 a month ($1,100 a year, rounded). But according to our budgets she would need $175 a month or $2,100 a year. At age 62, therefore, OASDI payments would be short $1,000 annually (Table 9).

We may recall that if all the protection were provided by private means, insurance in force of $67,000 for the USDL family and $87,000 for the OASDI family would be needed. Estimating supplements to OASDI is much more complicated than calculating the $67,000 and $87,000 was, because OASDI protection is not continuous (as was assumed in our other calculations), but intermittent — there is a gap in protection (and payments) from the time the youngest child is 18 until the widow reaches 62.

[25] Computed from United States Department of Labor data. Except for retail trade ($53.06 in 1955) other industry figures (annual earnings) hover around or are higher than manufacturing. The level of employment in retail trade is not sufficiently high so as to bias downward our computed $3,800.

[26] We are doing an injustice to exactness in using these rounded figures. A weekly wage of $75.70 would give monthly earnings yielding a benefit of $245.40.

Table 9. Comparison of Widow's Annual Needs and
OASDI Income, 1960

Age of Widow, Need, Amount Provided by OASDI, Difference	USDL Family		OASDI Family	
	1st 5 Yrs.	2nd 5 Yrs.	1st 15 Yrs.	2nd 2 Yrs.
Until 46				
Need	$4,500	$3,300		
Provided	3,000	2,300		
Difference ...	$1,500	$1,000		
46–62				
Need	$2,100			
Provided	0			
Difference ...	$2,100			
62 and over				
Need	$2,100			
Provided	1,100			
Difference ...	$1,000			
Until 42				
Need			$4,500	$3,300
Provided			3,000	2,300
Difference ...			$1,500	$1,000
42–62				
Need			$2,100	
Provided			0	
Difference ...			$2,100	
62 and over				
Need			$2,100	
Provided			1,100	
Difference ...			$1,000	

Two cases illustrate the supplements necessary to bring income up to the $4,500 level. These cases to not exhaust the possibilities, but they are realistic and relevant.

Case 1. Supplementary protection required until the youngest child is 18. The USDL family needs help for a total of 10 years: $4,500 for 5 years, of which OASDI provides $3,000, and $3,300 for another 5 years, of which OASDI provides $2,300.[27] The OASDI family needs the same except that the $4,500 is required for 15 years, then $3,300 for 2 years. At 3 per cent interest the lump sums are $11,000 for the USDL family and $19,400 for the OASDI family.[28]

[27] Recall that we are using rounded figures though this makes for a slight inexactness and error.

[28] If we use a 3¾ per cent interest rate (as we do in the illustrations in the third chapter, the costs become $10,600 and $18,300, respectively.

This means, according to the data in Table 8 (which shows in the third column plus the seventh column a total private accumulation of $17,100 in 1960) that the average USDL family has enough protection to meet a minimum budget after premature death, but the OASDI family falls slightly short.[29] But note the severe restraints imposed: from the time the widow is 46 (USDL) or 42 (OASDI) until she is 62 she has no public-program income; at 62 OASDI payments ($1,100 a year) begin again. It is easy to suggest that the widow get a job; family responsibilities are now absent, but the likelihood of her getting a job is quite another matter, even though she has secretarial, teaching, or other professional training. Age is critical.

Case 2. Supplementary protection required as under Case 1, and, in addition, $2,100 annually until the widow reaches 62 (really primary protection in these years), and then $1,000 annually until death. For the USDL family the cost of such supplementary protection is approximately $35,000; for the OASDI family, $45,000.[30]

Again referring to Table 8 with its total private 1960 accumulation of $17,100, protection is at 47 per cent for the USDL family and 36 per cent for the OASDI family, still far short of the ideal; but compared with a half century before, the degree of improvement is striking. Moreover, at present, protection is highest when needed: until the children are 18; when the widow's OASDI payments cease, she is much better equipped in this sense to go to work.

Let us summarize. In 1910, the average level of formal financial protection against premature death was about 10 per cent; for every $100 of need caused by premature death, about $10 was available. The rest would have to come informally from relatives, friends, or charity. In 1960 protection was approximately enough if we use the very severe assumptions of Case 1, but only between a third and a half for Case 2. Though an important part of the improvement was OASDI protection, private programs were also instrumental. All the residual programs, categorical (Aid to Dependent Children) and others (general public as-

[29] Each family has two children. Technically, therefore, the net equity figure should go to $8,600 from $4,300 and the total private accumulation should become $17,100 plus $4,300 or $21,400. In this situation both families have sufficient private accumulations to cover costs until the children are 18, after which their net equity share no longer stays with the family.

[30] These figures may sound high compared with the $11,000 or $19,400 of Case 1. But a lot more money is paid out; the OASDI widow, for example, receives $2,100 a year for 20 years. This is the costly part of the protection.

sistance), are excluded; we are concerned here with right rather than with need.

A Look at the Present Scene

If the improvement has been as marked as these figures suggest, one might ask whether there is still a problem and if so, why.

That there remains a problem is evident from studies during the last five years, perhaps the most revealing of them made by the Social Security Administration in the "Income of Young Survivors" series.[31] These studies suggest that survivors' incomes were less than the degree of protection we have described as existing would indicate. Our figures suggest that the average family under OASDI would, from social security and private means, be able to meet its $4,500 budget. The Social Security Administration studies name a median young-survivor income of $2,830 (1957), which includes income from employment. This figure is lower than that suggested by our data for a number of reasons.

First, protection is not evenly distributed. A nationwide survey conducted by units of the life insurance industry shows that about half of all men and women with a family income under $3,000 a year, about two thirds with incomes between $3,000 and $5,000, more than three fourths with incomes of $5,000 and over were insured.[32] The same pattern appears when one looks at the relation between annual income and face value of life insurance owned (Table 10).

The sizable difference between life insurance per family ($10,200 in 1960) and average death benefit (approximately $1,650 in 1960)[33] is explainable: insurance per family includes more than insurance on the life of the breadwinner only; all insurance proceeds are not paid out in one year; and there is some lag in accumulation — older people who bought their insurance years ago may have policies whose face value is below the median. It is pertinent nevertheless to note the average payout in relation to need, particularly if a considerable part of the payout

---

[31] See Mollie Orshansky, "Income of Young Survivors," *Social Security Bulletin*, September, 1959, pp. 10–15, 24. See also subsequent articles in the same *Bulletin*.

[32] *Life Insurance Fact Book, 1962*, New York: Institute of Life Insurance, p. 8.

[33] The first figure is from *ibid.*, p. 15; the second, *ibid.*, p. 44, and was obtained by dividing $3,346 billions in death benefits by 2,038 million payments. These 2,038 million payments were made to a smaller number of people, since one person might own policies in more than one company. The $1,650 might be increased by 50 per cent to give a more realistic per deceased figure. In 1957, life insurance per family was $8,300, not the $10,200 of 1960; this would also help to explain some of the variation.

can be regarded as being expended for burial costs and for settling the estate.

Though OASDI protection is distributed more evenly than life insurance, it also has certain characteristics that explain the gap between my data and the Social Security Administration's. OASDI coverage has broadened over the years; the 1957 survey included proportionately more families not covered by OASDI than there would have been in such a study in 1960. With broader coverage in 1960, one would expect the incomes of survivors to be higher in 1960 than before, apart from any upward movement in benefits. But such movement is also an important reason. Congress has periodically increased the benefits, markedly between 1957 and 1960. In 1957 the maximum family benefit was $2,400 a year; in 1958 it was raised to $3,048. A 1960 survey would have yielded results more compatible with our figures.

Table 10. Relation between Income * and Average Size of
Insurance Policy

Income	Average Size of Policy		
	Men	Women	Total
Under $3,000	$ 6,133	$ 2,050	$ 4,340
$3,000–$4,999	8,110	3,170	6,970
$5,000–$7,499	10,880	4,990	10,620
$7,500–$9,999	14,170		13,990
$10,000 and over	26,730	36,190	26,910
Average size	12,040	3,490	10,770

Source: *Life Insurance Buying, 1960*, New York: Institute of Life Insurance, 1961, p. 9.
* Those not gainfully employed excluded.

Finally, under OASDI, there are lags of various sorts because the benefit schedule is tied to earnings. Family benefits are related to the prior annual earnings of the deceased. Though such benefits increase if the benefit structure moves upward, it is also true that if the benefit maximums are increased (and these are related to higher earnings), the family of an already deceased person can qualify for the new maximum benefits only if the family is at the previous maximum.

But all these factors notwithstanding, it remains true that there *is* a gap between the ideal level of income maintenance and what is currently existent.

Today and Yesterday

As we did at the end of the last chapter, let us compare a modern man's protection with his grandfather's. Fifty years ago protection tended to be nonincome, implicitly-provided service, with families playing an important role. Today it is impersonal, explicit, income-oriented. In earlier times the government played a small part, entering with welfare measures only as a last resort. Today through OASDI government is the first line of support for most of the population. In 1910, explicit income probably provided not more than 10 per cent of the minimum budget; today the figure is closer to 30 or 40 per cent, and over the short run (until the children are 18) near 60 per cent.

Indexes of Insecurity and Security; Policy Comments

Indexes of insecurity and security for 1910 and 1960 provide no clues to the qualitative characteristics of insecurity and security, but they provide numbers which may be of interest (Table 11). We must re-

Table 11. Aggregate Indexes of Economic Insecurity and Security in Premature Death

	Ideal	1910	1960	2010
The Insecurity: Premature Death				
Frequency: probability at age 14 of dying before 65	0%	47%	27%	?%
Severity	0%		Gentle upward drift	
The Security: Protection against Premature Death *				
Short-run alleviation as percentage of nondeferrable budget †				
Public programs: income as a matter of right	67%	0	30%	40%
Private programs and private means; income as a matter of right.	33%	5–10%	33%	45%
Total	100%	5–10%	63%	85%
Long-run alleviation as percentage of nondeferrable budget ‡				
Public programs: income as a matter of right	50%	0	15%	15%
Private programs and private means; income as a matter of right.	50%	<5%	25%	35%
Total	100%	<5%	40%	50%

* These are global data and apply to *all* those left behind by premature death, whether or not individually covered by public and/or private programs.

† Until children are 18 for the total group of survivors of those dying prematurely.

‡ After children are 18 and until widow reaches retirement age or has a change of status such as remarriage.

member first that these indexes are partly subjective, though this does not mean they are arbitrary or capricious. Moreover, the ideals of 0% or 100% should be viewed conservatively: though empirically it may never be possible to reduce premature death to 0% it is not abstractly impossible, and it is desirable. Similarly, the ideal of meeting the family's budgetary needs completely does not mean meeting any budget however large, but rather meeting the standard. Finally, our security index takes into account only explicit income arising independently, not implicit aid forthcoming if, for example, the family moves in with grandparents after the husband is dead.

In the following chapters, dealing with old age, unemployment, accidental injury and sickness, considerable space will be devoted to policy suggestions; here the problems appear less complex and the discussion can be simpler.

A satisfactory socioeconomic mechanism exists at present for meeting the problems of premature death, and, with some reservations, people generally accept this mechanism. This system includes the government, which provides a floor of protection; employers, labor organizations, and others, who put a layer of carpeting on the floor with group insurance; and individuals themselves, who provide a second layer of carpeting — insurance and savings. The government may enter at other stages; if, for example, a floor of protection is not provided through OASDI and help is required, categorical aid programs or general assistance may be offered. A formal public and private framework for providing protection exists.

Two problems remain: one is to extend the programs to cover those not now covered; universal OASDI coverage is increasingly a reality; private programs are encouraging, though compulsion is antithetical to private action. The second problem is that needs are not being met. But distinct improvement can be observed (recall the comparison of 1960 with 1910), and with continued economic growth one may expect continued improvement at a rate faster than that of the last half century. One may doubt that it will ever reach the stage where needs are fully met, but I believe we come closer to it year by year. More important, acute poverty appears to be much less of a problem now than in 1910.

Though man does not live by it alone, bread is critically important and we have been doing a better job of providing it for surviving fami-

41

lies after premature death by means of satisfactory basic programs. The major issue now is the quantity of resources. Society and its individual members have made these choices; in the future we shall probably choose to put aside proportionately more of a rising real income to prevent the undesirable consequences of premature death.

■ OLD AGE

PREMATURE death is dying too soon, and old age, in the same context, is living too long: not too long in psychological or physiological terms, but too long in economic terms — outliving one's means of livelihood.

If one dies leaving no economic obligations unmet, premature death in our sense is not applicable, as we saw earlier. Similarly, if one dies with his working boots on, "old age" does not apply. But the old-age problem is more complex in various ways than premature death is.[1]

In the real world, many people do not die prematurely; they live too long. But both dying too soon and living too long are difficult to measure abstractly. Earlier I called all deaths before 65 and after 14 possibly premature; similarly one may view all living past 65 as allowing the possibility of living too long. One way of meeting premature death is prevention — keeping the person alive, but the old age equivalent is hardly death at 65, though of course that is a "solution," for if you do not live beyond retirement you can hardly outlive your income. Other means than death at 65 must be employed, and we shall examine them later in this chapter.

Chronological Frequency

The problem is as frequent as is age 65; all who do not die prematurely live to face the opposite problem. But beyond this, the old-age problem differs from that of premature death. The very fact of premature death brings into existence the insecurity; the loss of the breadwinner means

[1] Although organized materials on premature death are hard to find, an abundance exists for old age. Three useful source volumes are John J. Corson and John W. McConnell, *Economic Needs of Older People*, New York: Twentieth Century Fund, 1956; Peter O. Steiner and Robert Dorfman, *The Economic Status of the Aged*, Berkeley: University of California Press, 1957; and Clark Tibbitts, ed., *Aging and Society: A Handbook of Social Gerontology*, Chicago: University of Chicago Press, 1960, especially the chapter "Aging and Income Security" by Margaret S. Gordon. A sizable quantity of useful materials has come from Congressional hearings; much of this is available in printed form.

43

Table 12. Survivorship and Life Expectancy at Age 65 for Selected Periods

Year	Surviving from 100,000 Born Alive				Average No. of Years of Life Remaining			
	Male		Female		Male		Female	
	White	Nonwhite	White	Nonwhite	White	Nonwhite	White	Nonwhite
1900–02	39,245	19,015	43,806	21,995	11.51	10.38	12.23	11.38
1909–11	40,862	17,806	47,086	22,302	11.25	9.74	11.97	10.82
1919–21	50,663	34,042	54,299	31,044	12.21	12.07	12.75	12.41
1929–31	52,964	29,314	60,499	30,852	11.77	10.87	12.81	12.24
1939–41	58,305	35,912	68,701	40,718	12.07	12.18	13.56	13.95
1949–51	63,541	45,198	76,773	52,358	12.75	12.75	15.00	14.54
1959	65,853	50,300	80,801	60,298	12.7	12.5	15.6	15.2

Source: *Vital Statistics of the United States, 1959,* United States Department of Health, Education, and Welfare, Public Health Service, National Office of Vital Statistics, Vol. 1, Table 5C, pp. 5–7.

loss of income — insecurity. In old age the parallel is not quite exact: reaching 65 does not necessarily mean retiring and losing income.

Table 12 gives information about the numbers (out of 100,000) reaching 65 and life expectancy. Two facts leap out at one from this table: the great increase in the numbers reaching age 65 (and the concomitant absolute increase in the numbers facing old age) and the very slight increase in life expectancy at age 65. One could therefore conclude that today greater numbers of people than ever before are reaching 65 and facing old age, but that for this increased number, life expectancy is not much greater than it was a half century ago. Of course, every reduction in premature death increases the likelihood of still greater numbers' reaching 65, and every medical advance that reduces the degenerative diseases of old age increases life expectancy. Table 13 shows in both

Table 13. Absolute Numbers and Percentages of Males and Females 65 and Over in 1910, 1960, and 1980

Year	Male		Female	
	No.	% of Total Male Pop.	No.	% of Total Female Pop.
1910	1,986,000	4.2	1,963,000	4.4
1960	7,501,000	8.5	9,057,000	10.0
1980 (projected) ..	10,267,000	8.5	14,259,000	11.5

Sources: *Thirteenth Census of the United States, 1910; Current Population Reports*, United States Department of Commerce, Bureau of the Census (Series P-25, No. 187); and *United States Census of Population, 1960.*

Table 14. Additional Years of Life that Can Be Expected by Males and Females 65, by Sex, 1939–41, 1949–51, and 2000

Year	No. of Additional Years	
	Male	Female
1939–41	12.07	13.57
1949–51	12.74	14.95
2000		
Low mortality	16.11	18.39
High mortality	13.80	16.69

Source: *Illustrative United States Population Projections*, United States Department of Health, Education, and Welfare, Social Security Administration, Division of the Actuary (Actuarial Study No. 46), May, 1957, p. 15.

absolute numbers and percentages the increased numbers of people reaching 65, and Table 14 presents several projections of life expectancy.

Table 15 shows the marital status and Table 16 the living arrangements of the aging fifty years ago and today. The proportion of widows is far greater than that of widowers (which arises out of differences in longevity and which creates employment and maintenance problems to be discussed below). But this pattern has stayed much the same during the half century, though the proportion of the widowed has fallen and that of the divorced has risen. Unmarried men have tended to live less in families and more in institutions, revealing the greater willingness of

Table 15. Marital Status of Males and Females
65 and Over in 1910 and 1960

Year and Status	% of Males	% of Females
1910		
Never married	6.2	6.3
Married and living with spouse	65.6	35.0
Widowed	27.1	58.1
Divorced	0.7	0.4
1960		
Never married	6.3	7.4
Married and living with spouse	69.6	35.7
Widowed	20.3	53.4
Divorced	3.8	3.4

Source: Constructed from data in the censuses of population for the years 1910 and 1960.

Table 16. Living Arrangements of Unmarried Males
and Females 65 and Over in 1910 and 1960

Year and Arrangement	% of Males	% of Females
1910		
In families	>50–55	>50–55
Alone or in lodgings	<35–40	<35–40
In institutions	>10	>10
1960		
In families	44.1	48.4
Alone or in lodgings	44.9	45.0
In institutions	11.0	6.2

Source: Constructed from data in the censuses of population for the years 1910 and 1960.

families to take in old women. There has been a decided decrease in living with one's children, a decrease in living in institutions, and an increase in living alone. This reflects, in part at least, the growth of independent and explicit income such as that provided by OASDI.

Frequency of Unemployment

The above data show increases — absolute and relative — in the numbers of persons 65 and over, and less marked changes in marital status or living arrangements. There has been an increase in the number of the aged. But if these old people all kept on working (in the extreme case, until death), what appears to be a more frequent problem would in fact not be. Once, years ago, it could be "safely assumed that all but a handful [of those over 60 or 65] would continue in gainful employment until stricken by death or serious disability. For most men, a distinction between the prospective . . . life span and the length of working life would . . . have been meaningless." [2] Table 17 illustrates this, and points up the growth of retirement life expectancy, which creates the very problem we are talking about: remaining years without remaining employment. We use age 60 here rather than 65 because it presents the issues more strikingly.

Over the years there is a marked decrease in the employment of older people, compounding the frequency of the problem: more older people, fewer at work (Table 18).

Table 17. Life and Retirement Expectancy for Persons
60 in 1900, 1955, and 1975

| Year | Expectancy | | | Retirement as Percentage of Total Life |
	Total Life	Work Life	Retirement Life	
1900	14.3	11.5	2.8	20
1955	15.9	9.2	6.7	42
1975	17.2	9.0	8.2	48

Source: *Tables of Working Life*, United States Department of Labor, Bureau of Labor Statistics (Bulletin No. 1001), 1950.

What appears to be an anomaly — the figures in the first column increasing, those in the second decreasing — is not one. Older people have

[2] *Tables of Working Life*, United States Department of Labor, Bureau of Labor Statistics, Bulletin No. 1001, 1950, p. 3.

Table 18. Data on Persons 65 and Over in Labor Force,
1900, 1950, 1960, and 1975

	65+ as % of Total Labor Force	% of 65+ in Labor Force (Participation Rate)	
		Male	Female
1900	3.9	63.2	8.3
1950	4.9	45.8	9.7
1960	4.8	32.3	10.5
1975	4.7	31.0	12.6

Sources: *Historical Statistics of the United States 1789–1957*, *Statistical Abstract of the United States,* and Sophia Cooper, *Labor Force Projections to 1975,* United States Department of Labor, Bureau of Labor Statistics (Reprint No. 2268), 1958.

been increasing relative to the rest of the population (and to the labor force), and even though relatively fewer of these old people are working (their participation rate has gone down), there are enough more of them relative to the rest of the labor force to raise the rate from 3.9 in 1900 to 4.8 in 1960. World War II's manpower demands temporarily checked the drop in the participation rate of the aged: in 1940 the rate for males was 45.0, in 1945 49.9. By 1950 it was down to 45.8 again, and, except for another leveling during the Korean period, it has since steadily declined. Owing to changes in women's status, their experience has been slightly different; the third column of Table 18 does not parallel the second.

One may draw these conclusions: There are more 65-year-olds now than earlier; the frequency of the problem has increased, both absolutely and relatively. Life expectancy for those reaching 65 is not much greater than it was a generation ago. But whereas a generation or two ago there was little distinction between the prospective life span and the length of working life, such a distinction is most definitely made today: people retire, but they live on for some years afterward, causing the problem of maintaining income. And if less than a third of the men 65 and over are in the labor force, the income problem may be said to exist for two of each three men over 65. Moreover, the frequency of the problem becomes greater with increasing age.

Severity

The economic frequency of the old-age problem may be looked at as a combination of age and interruption of income; i.e., frequency can be looked at from the income side of the ledger. On the opposite side, the expense side, even if income is curtailed, if expenses also decline the problem may be less severe. In premature death, the expenses dropped immediately because there is one fewer family member to support.

The first, and most obvious, difference in the expense patterns for the elderly is that one member does not die: hence at first blush the problem seems compounded: income is lowered while there remain the same bodies to clothe and mouths to feed. But a set of forces gradually lower needs as age advances: the children grow up and depart; the mortgage gets paid off; the pressure to keep up with the Joneses diminishes. Against these operate forces to increase expenses, the most obvious being medical care as illness happens oftener and more severely. As we shall see later (pp. 123–124) the treatment of disease has itself become more costly; the rise in the medical-cost components of price indexes has been among the steepest of all components since 1945.

Quantitatively each person's experience varies; but though it is interesting to examine individual case histories, it can be difficult to generalize from them. Various kinds of budgets have been developed to circumvent this difficulty, leaving one with the task of examining the items included in the budgets and their prices.

In the last two decades both the United States Department of Labor and the Social Security Administration have developed standard budgets, of which we have encountered two — the USDL and the OASDI (pp. 30–32). Here we shall look at another Social Security Administration budget, the "Budget for an Elderly Couple." [3]

The 1945–48 version of this budget — the first — was designed to "provide a modest but adequate living standard." Priced out annually for thirty-four cities it approximated a low of $1,600 (New Orleans) and a high of $1,900 (Milwaukee). With the highly variable costs of

[3] For a detailed discussion see Mollie Orshansky, "Budget for an Elderly Couple: Interim Revision by the Bureau of Labor Statistics," *Social Security Bulletin*, December, 1960, pp. 26–36. See also earlier discussions by Lenore Epstein in the same journal.

Budgets of this kind are not without their controversial aspects; the article by Mollie Orshansky spells out a number of these. For example, should a car be included for the elderly couple? In the 1959 upgrading, it was included for an estimated 22 per cent of the families. What kinds of adjustment should be made if the food component is scaled up or down? These problems (and intercity differences) notwithstanding, such budgets *are* useful. For a technical discussion see "Statement of Ewan Clague" in United States Congress, United States Senate, Special Committee on Aging, *Hearings before the Subcommittee on Retirement Income of the Aging: Retirement Income of the Aging* (84th Congress, 1st Session, 1961).

housing, heat, and utilities excluded, the low budget was $1,125 (Savannah) and the high $1,270 (Seattle). The budget was updated late in 1959, and for twenty large cities it ranged from a low of $2,641 (Houston) to a high of $3,366 (Chicago). This budget was also upgraded: the increase in 1959 over 1945–48 represented not only mere changes in prices but also a higher standard of living. Had the old budget been priced out in 1959, it would have ranged from $2,390 (Houston) to $3,112 (Chicago). (Table 19.)

Table 19. Budgets for Elderly Couple (1948, 1959) and City Worker (1959)

Type of Family Unit, Date, and No. of Cities	Budget in High-Cost City	Budget in Low-Cost City
Elderly couple		
1948, 34 cities	$1,900 (Milwaukee)	$1,600 (New Orleans)
Autumn, 1959, 20 cities, same		
budget repriced	3,102 (Chicago)	2,390 (Houston)
Autumn, 1959, 20 cities, revised		
budget	3,366 (Chicago)	2,641 (Houston)
City Worker		
Autumn, 1959, 20 cities	6,567 (Chicago)	5,370 (Houston)

Source: *Social Security Bulletin*, December, 1960, pp. 29–30.

We turn to a then-and-now comparison — the budget for an elderly couple half a century ago and at present — because we want to look at changes in the patterns of insecurity and the adjustment to them. Though it is not possible to discover all the components of the several budgets available for early in the century, total dollar amounts are obtainable (Tables 20 and 21). In spite of some discrepancy in the two sets of figures, the families category in Table 21 fits closely with the 1911 family-of-five class in Table 20. The budget for the couples in Table 21 is lower than that for the elderly couple of Table 20; it is my belief that the elderly couple's decent standard budget of Table 20 is the more realistic, for two reasons: the Massachusetts data are for the aged poor, causing a downward bias in the budgets of Table 21; and we have incorporated 1913 and 1914 data into constructing the budget, causing an upward bias in the elderly couple figures in Table 20. There was less difference between elderly couple and family budgets in 1910 than we find today: in 1960 the elderly couple's budget was half of the city worker's (the worker's family including only two children); in

Table 20. Family Budgets in 1910, 1911, 1913, and 1914

Size of Family, Date, and Standard	South		North	
	Rural	Urban	Rural	Urban
5 persons				
1911, extremely low*..		$600		$650
1913, fair†	$650		$750	$850
1914, decent‡		$775 (est.)		$825
Couple, elderly				
1910, decent§		$600		$550

Source: As cited in Abraham Epstein, *Facing Old Age*, New York: Knopf, 1922, Ch. 6.
* F. H. Streightoff, as cited in Epstein.
† Scott Nearing, as cited in Epstein.
‡ J. H. Hollander, as cited in Epstein.
§ Adjusted by the writer from the Hollander and Scott Nearing budgets by assuming that food and clothing costs could be decreased by ⅖, other costs by ⅕.

Table 21. Weekly and Annual Average Expenditures for
All Purposes by the Nondependent Aged Poor in
Massachusetts in 1910

Category	Average Weekly Expenditure	Average Annual Expenditure
Individual males	$ 6.25	$325.00
Individual females	4.28	223.00
Couples	9.32	485.00
Families	12.00	624.00

Source: Lee Willing Squier, *Old Age Dependency in the United States*, New York: Macmillan, 1912, Ch. 1.

Table 22. Elderly Couples' Budgets in 1910 and 1960,
North and South, in Current Dollars and
in 1947–49 Dollars

Year	North	South
	Current Dollars	
1910	$ 600	$ 550
1959 (Autumn) ...	$3,366 (Chicago)	$2,641 (Houston)
	1947–49 Dollars	
1910	$1,481	$1,355
1960	$2,654	$2,197

Source: Adapted from Tables 19, 20, and 21.

1910 the elderly couple's budget was about three fourths of the family budget (the family including three children).

Table 22 summarizes the 1910 and 1960 budgets in both current and standard (1947–49) dollars. Again, though such conversions must be interpreted cautiously, we believe they shed light on the changing patterns.

Today and Yesterday

Compared with my father's and grandfather's, my old-age outlook can be summarized briefly.

There are more people today — absolutely and relatively — than in either of the two preceding generations; the aggregate problem is therefore compounded. Life expectancy at age 65 today is not much greater than for either one's father or grandfather: if one were 65, it would be about 13 years, for his father at 65, approximately 12, for his grandfather at 65, 11.

As a matter of fact, my forebears did not achieve these averages; my father died at 72, 5 years short; my two grandfathers at 66 and 67, or about a decade short. But all three of them died while they were still working.

But if life expectancy has not increased much, the retirement phase of it has: I can expect about 8 years, my forebears expected 5 and 3 years respectively. I am less likely to be in the labor force after 65 than were either my father or grandfathers. My grandfathers would have had two chances out of three of being in the labor force after 65; mine are one out of three or fewer.

I am less likely to be living with my children or other relatives or in an institution after 65 than were my parents or grandparents. I am more likely to have my own house and live there with my wife but no others. The probability still is that I will die before my wife. (In 1961, 29.5 per cent of the females 65 and over were widows; only 9.1 per cent of the males were widowers.)

In current dollars, an elderly couple's budget for my wife and me would be $3,350 in the North and $2,650 in the South. Allowing for changes in the value of the dollar, this is over one and a half times the budget for my grandparents. There is little doubt that part of this increase (in real terms) is owing to an upgraded budget; older people today live at a real level higher than those of several generations ago.

The Preventive Ideal and Current Reality

The ideal solution to the economic problems of old age might be either work for those able and willing to work or income maintenance at a budgetarily acceptable level for those unable or unwilling. The first choice is not generally available, and the second, with variations in the meaning of budgetarily acceptable, is much more the rule.

Compulsory retirement at 65 or 62 is the rule for a complex set of economic, administrative, and social reasons; to explore them is to begin to find out what can be done about widening the income maintenance choices of the older person. The major limitations on the job possibilities of the able and willing older person are listed below.

Over the last fifty to one hundred years the economy has shifted from self-employment or working for a small business to working, as over four fifths of us do, for someone else, often for a big employer. A self-employed craftsman might go on working as long as his health and economic circumstances permitted; an employee of a large corporation would not be expected to have this freedom. The decline of agriculture — in which self-employment was so large and where the older person could be useful — exemplifies this kind of change.

Even though most of us work for others, it is conceivable that the older employee might still have a particular kind of usefulness to the employer and be kept on in his later years. But the older-worker problem has been compounded by a changing technology that operates in favor of the younger person; job content and job requirements have altered to put the older worker at a disadvantage. Whether the impact of automation will change the trend remains to be seen; certainly at existing technological levels the older worker appears less valuable to his employer.

Accompanying these two facts has been a movement of the population away from the country to the city, heightening the problem, though this is not an independent force. If opportunities for employing the older worker are greater on the farm or in the small town but old people are increasingly found in the city, it is idle to speculate on what might have been (or what might be).

Even if the aforementioned facts encouraged rather than impeded the employment of older persons, one economic force might well be sufficient to counteract them; added to them, it doubly compounds the problem. This economic force is the lump-of-labor thesis: there are just so

53

many jobs to go around, and one way the young person can be sure of getting work is to retire the older person and open up the job. This theory was given added impetus during the great depression, as one can corroborate by reading the legislative history of the Social Security Act or the Fair Labor Standards Act (with its overtime premium as another testimonial to the theory) or, more importantly, the Railroad Retirement Act of 1934, which included certain conditions making retirement at 65 almost compulsory (by prohibitive reductions for deferred retirement).[4] Logical or not, the belief persists as a basis for action, appearing now and again during recessions in the 1950's and up to the present.

All the above facts point to the decreasing usefulness of the older worker and the belief that he should be retired. The result has been compulsory retirement at 65, which becomes another deterrent to continued employment. The age chosen is 65 for many reasons — some actuarial, some cultural, some operational — which surrounded the deliberations of the Committee on Economic Security and other groups in the mid-thirties, when this cut-off age crystallized. Administrative simplicity is the reason for making retirement compulsory.

There are some less effective forces keeping older people at work. Some people — possibly an increasing number — believe that a person should have the right to keep on working if he wants to. More important, some believe that the economy may not be able to afford, in real terms, the increasing burden of relatively growing numbers of older people. And some believe that if we get into something warmer than a cold war, everyone's services will be needed.

The chances of successfully solving the old-age economic insecurity problem through continued employment are not very great, for four reasons.[5] First, the health of the older people prevents many from working. Even in years of peak employment a third or more of the retired people over 65 are unable to work gainfully.[6] Second, despite an abundance of studies showing the efficiency, high morale, and other virtues of older workers, our technology is not well suited to their continued em-

[4] I am indebted to Robert J. Myers for this illustration.

[5] For balanced presentations on this problem see Corson and McConnell, *op. cit.*, Ch. 3; and *Employment of the Older Worker*, Kalamazoo: W. E. Upjohn Institute for Employment Research, 1959. There is a vast quantity of material currently pouring out on this topic.

[6] Edna C. Wentworth, "Disabled Old-Age Insurance Beneficiaries," *Social Security Bulletin*, June, 1951, pp. 11–12.

ployment. If one adds to this increasing severity if not frequency of accidents, increasing illness and absence from the job, and increasing costs such as insurance, it is unlikely that one will find wide employment of older workers as a solution to the problem. Third, though some employers and some unions show genuine interest in continued employment, there is a beautiful simplicity about compulsory retirement at a fixed age. By contrast, selective and individual retirement requires all kinds of decisions and raises the possibility of discrimination. At the risk of committing heresy against classical economics, I suspect there is a germ of truth in the lump-of-labor thesis or at least in some kind of underutilization thesis. This acts — and I believe it will continue to act — as a spur to get the older person out of the labor force, and will persist as long as unemployment is at 5 or 6 per cent. I strongly support measures and programs designed to meet the economic insecurity problems of the aged through continued employment, but I am not sanguine about their success.

Employing the Aged

Having expressed the beliefs above, the analysis now turns to the facts. The accompanying tabulation, which enlarges upon the data of Table 18, assumes that the labor force participation rate, from 1890 to 1975, is equal to employment at wage levels permitting budgets to be met. The problem would be harder if the old person were employed at wages or hours insufficient to allow him to exist.

	Male	Female		Male	Female
1890	68.3%	7.3%	1950	41.4	9.7
1900	63.2	8.3	1960	32.3	10.5
1920	55.6	7.3	1965	34.0	11.7
1930	54.0	7.3	1970	32.1	12.2
1940	42.2	6.0	1975	31.0	12.6

Two thirds of the males, a half century ago, were part of the labor force; by 1960 the figure had dropped to a third. For females the trend has been different: from 8 per cent in 1900 to over 10 per cent currently. (Data for years after 1960 show approximately 30 per cent for males.) By subgroups the picture is more marked, as shown in the accompanying tabulation of those working in 1950.[7]

On page 48 we equated the 65-and-over participation rate with employment and assumed that all those in the labor force were at work and

[7] See Corson and McConnell, *op. cit.*, p. 49.

In Labor Force

Men

    65–69 .... 57.1%

    70–74 .... 39.6

    75 and over 19.3

Women

    65–69 .... 16.0

    70–74 .... 7.5

    75 and over 3.0

providing for themselves by that employment. With respect to earnings, the assumption is wide of the mark, in 1960, for males by some 5 per cent, and by some 4 per cent for females; of men 65 and over in the labor force some 5 per cent were unemployed in late 1960, and 4 per cent of the women.[8] In late 1960, these 4 and 5 per cent unemployment rates were not excessively high compared with rates for other ages: between 3 and 4 per cent for men and women 35–54, but over 10 per cent for those 14–19, and close to 9 (males) and 7 (females) for those 20–24.[9]

A more likely cause for concern is that many over 65, once retired, believe their chances of finding a new job are so dismal that they simply take themselves out of the labor force. Fewer than a third of the men 65 and over and approximately a tenth of the women provide for their security through continued employment; the figures are higher for immediately after 65; of males 65–69, over fifty per cent were employed; of those 70–74, less than forty, and of those 75 and over, less than twenty. The proportions are similar for women.

Are the earnings of those employed sufficient to meet requirements? A 1960 study shows that the median income of men working full time for 50–52 weeks was $4,120.[10] A 1958 study revealed that fully employed veterans had a median income of $4,350, nonveterans, $3,255; data on part-time earnings were not available. One might assume that the earnings were sufficient.

We noted that in current dollars an old-age budget approximated $600 in 1910–15. A study by Paul H. Douglas says that in 1910 average annual earnings in all industries including farm labor were $574; exclud-

[8] Hence if one were to equate participation rate with employment, the former should be corrected by the unemployment rate. To do this, multiply the participation rate by the unemployment rate and subtract the product from the former.

[9] For data of these varieties see the "Monthly Report on the Labor Force," as contained in *Employment and Earnings,* a publication of the United States Department of Labor.

[10] Lenore A. Epstein, "Sources and Size of Money Income of the Aged," *Social Security Bulletin,* January, 1962, p. 16.

ing farm labor, $630.[11] These data are for employees of *all* ages; how much they need to be adjusted downward for the older worker is not certain. Some analysts have suggested a problem: Abraham Epstein, for example, wrote in 1922 a chapter called "The Chasm between the Cost of Living and Wages."[12] We would hazard that in 1910 the expenses of the older person (or couple) declined more than income did, and wages therefore approximately met budgetary requirements.

My chance of supporting myself by continuing to work in my old age is likely to be less than a third, for my father it was between a third and a half, and for my grandfather closer to sixty per cent. There is a sizable variation depending not only upon the person and his health but also upon his occupation. A healthy person in agriculture or the professions can count on much greater employment opportunities than can one in mining, manufacturing, and transportation, where fewer than 2 per cent of the employees are 65 or over. As to the wages of the older workers, both in 1910 and 1960 they seemed sufficient to cover normal needs. The real problem was not and is not the level of earnings for those employed, but getting a job. All this points to the need for alternative means of maintaining income.

The Alleviative Ideal and Current Reality

We start with the proposition that some three fourths of the aged or their dependents are not employed — have no income from work and need alternative means of getting money. Moreover, some of the aged employed may need wages or supplements to their salaries.

Let us, for ease of calculation, strike a rough average of $3,000 as the mean between the 1960 elderly-couple budget high of $3,366 for Chicago and low of $2,641 for Houston. Further, we shall assume that we want a joint-and-survivor annuity kind of program, providing $3,000 a year for the couple (husband 65, wife 60) until the death of the husband, after which $2,100 a year is provided for the widow, with all payments ceasing at her death and no refunds to anyone.

One may suggest that of the various means of supplying these nonde-ferrable expenses government programs with as wide coverage as is fea-

---

[11] *Real Wages in the United States, 1890–1926*, Boston: Houghton Mifflin, 1930, Table 147, following p. 392. Later studies by Albert Rees would alter the Douglas data for manufacturing, but would not, in our judgment, change fundamentally the above figures.

[12] *Facing Old Age*, New York: Knopf, 1922, Ch. 6.

sible should provide half, with group and individual pensions plus other private means making up the balance.

The pure premium of one insurance company — using 1960 interest rates and mortality data — gives $48,000 as the capital sum needed to provide an annual income of first $3,000 and then $2,100 under these circumstances. To this would need to be added a loading or expense charge of about 2 per cent. One would run grave risks if one sought to self-insure here so as to save the insurance company charge, for if either husband or wife outlived his life expectancy, the income would be insufficient. But the $48,000 could be accumulated over a lifetime at a rate depending on the age at which one starts, the rate of interest, and whether there is capital appreciation. If we assume no capital appreciation and an interest rate of $3\frac{3}{4}$ per cent (in 1960 perhaps halfway between the conventional 3 per cent and the $4\frac{1}{2}$ per cent available from many credit unions), one would have to save $29 a month starting at age 20, $53 at 30, $91 at 40, and $187 at 50.

All of the less than three fourths of the aged population who are not working need not, at present, have such a capital sum on hand to provide an annual income, because a floor of protection is afforded by the Old Age and Survivors program of the Social Security Act. Table 23 shows that some 8.4 per cent of those 65 and over in 1960 had no income from present or previous employment or from public programs; another 2.0 per cent collected veterans' benefits; still another 9.2 per cent public assistance (in both cases with no earnings or other public income). To these groups we shall return later.

The employed group was 24.2 per cent of those 65 and over. We shall assume with some reason that persons in all three of the subcategories — about a quarter of the aged — in this group receive sufficient income to meet the elderly-couple budget; they have, that is, no income maintenance problem.

This leaves a little more than half the aged with social insurance benefits only. In 1960 the average monthly benefit to a retired worker and aged wife was $123.90, or annually, about $1,500, which means that social insurance meets approximately half of the elderly-couple budget. Instead of the $48,000 required to provide $3,000 a year, about half is needed to provide $1,500 annually.

In 1960 it was estimated that about one and a third million people were receiving private pensions and some six hundred thousand had

Table 23. Total Population and Males and Females in the United States, District of
Columbia, Puerto Rico, and the Virgin Islands, with Money Income
from Employment or Public Programs in December, 1960

Type of Income	Total Population		Males	Females
	Number	%		
Population 65 and over	16,960,000	100.0	7,690,000	9,270,000
Total employed*	4,110,000	24.2	2,330,000	1,780,000
No income from public programs	1,160,000	6.9	850,000	310,000
Social insurance benefits	2,550,000	15.0	1,220,000	1,330,000
Other public programs	400,000	2.3	260,000	140,000
Total retirement and survivor benefits†	12,010,000	70.8	5,770,000	6,240,000
No earnings or veterans' or public assistance payments ...	7,700,000	45.4	3,560,000	4,140,000
Veterans' payments	1,020,000	6.0	680,000	340,000
Public assistance	740,000	4.4	310,000	430,000
Total veterans' pension or compensation‡	1,670,000	9.8	990,000	680,000
No earnings or social insurance.	340,000	2.0	110,000	230,000
Total public assistance§	2,410,000	14.2	830,000	1,580,000
No earnings or payments under other public programs	1,560,000	9.2	450,000	1,110,000
No income from employment or public programs	1,490,000	8.4	250,000	1,240,000

Source: *Social Security Bulletin*, July, 1961, p. 7.

* Includes 3,220,000 earners and an estimated 890,000 nonworking wives of earners.

† Includes persons with income from one or more of the following sources: old-age, survivors, and disability insurance, railroad retirement, and government employees retirement. Excludes persons with benefits under unemployment or temporary disability insurance or workmen's compensation programs. Includes estimated number of beneficiaries' wives not in direct receipt of benefits.

‡ Includes a small number receiving supplementary public assistance.

§ Old-age assistance recipients and persons 65 and over receiving aid to the blind or to the permanently and totally disabled, including a small number receiving vendor payments for medical care but no direct cash payment either under old-age assistance or medical assistance for the aged.

income from annuities bought individually or elected as settlements under life insurance policies. The first group probably also were social insurance beneficiaries. If one assumes that OASDI plus a private pension permits reaching the elderly-couple goal, then another one and three tenths million should be added to the group above work to meet their budgets, reducing the social-insurance segment from over half to about 45 per cent. These facts are set forth in the accompanying tabulation.

Let us now look more closely at these last two cases. A little less than half the aged received about half their money from social insurance. If

Budget met through earnings, social insurance, and private pensions............35%
Half of budget met through social insurance 45%
No contributions to budget from employment or social insurance pensions......20%

we assume, as we did in the last chapter, that the average individual insurance and other assets (at face value) totaled $15,143, then a major
part of the balance needed is provided from these accumulations. Apart
from its reliance upon averages, there is, however, a limitation to this
reasoning: it assumes that insurance is carried at face value to 65 and
that it can then be converted to its face value. Neither of these assumptions is true: the amount of insurance carried at age 65 is less than the
average, since the need has decreased, and the average policy is not paid
up at 65, and hence cannot be converted at face value.[13]

A reduced asset figure is therefore necessary; an average capital accumulation of $12,000 might be more realistic (see below, pp. 131–132,
for the dangers of using averages). If all of it could be converted into
annuities, it would provide about $750 a year (applying the annuity
formula previously given). Thus, the elderly couple budget is short approximately $750 a year — $62.50 a month, a shortage of about 25 per
cent. In the premature death cases in Table 9 it was about 33⅓ per cent.
This advantage to the elderly couple appears to result from a relatively
lower budget, on the one hand, and relatively higher returns under
OASDI to the primary beneficiary, on the other. The remaining shortage is to be made up by a variety of means, from tightening one's belt
at one extreme through help from friends and relatives to old-age assistance at the other.

The 20 per cent who are neither employed nor receiving social insurance benefits — like those persons in the category above — might also
have assets of about $12,000, which would supply about a fourth of their
budget. As for the balance, Table 23 suggests that a small group —
about 300,000 persons (2 per cent of the aged) — receive money only
under veterans' programs. Another 1.6 million (about 9 per cent of the
aged) get public assistance. Finally, another 1.5 (about 8 per cent)
have no income from employment or public programs.

---

[13] After looking at the first draft of this manuscript, a reader asked why I did not
include annuity accumulations among the assets of older persons. The answers are that
procedurally I have done so in the above discussion and that conceptually annuities
are not capital accumulations at 65 — they are converted to current income streams.

It is difficult to draw any specific conclusions about the adequacy of the incomes of this 20 per cent. One might suggest, however, the following. First, the 1.5 million with no income from either employment or public programs are somehow provided for, though perhaps at a grinding subsistence level — in institutions or helped by friends and relatives as often as they are independent. The group getting public assistance may also be presumed to be adequately covered, though their incomes are maintained on the basis of need rather than right. The small group of veterans is more difficult to appraise.

A half century ago, as we saw earlier, the budget for an elderly couple was between $550 and $600 in current dollars. At that time social insurance programs were nonexistent, company pensions few, and individual annuities limited. But the possibility of continuing to work was much greater. The relative amount of institutional care was higher, as was public assistance to the aged, and relatives and friends played a more important part.

If we assume, as we did earlier (pp. 56–57), that the income of the two thirds of the older persons who were employed around 1910 was sufficient to meet their budgets, we are left still with the remaining third. Roughly, money income from all sources was probably between $75 and $100 a year — that is, it met only about a sixth of the budget (and this estimate may be high).

Table 24 is an index of economic security and insecurity for old age.

Though the preceding discussion understates the 1960 income-maintenance problems of the aged it overstates the problem for the future. The current problem is understated for at least two reasons. On the income side we have been dealing in averages, which tend to distort reality: For example, in 1960, the median money income of a family of two with a head aged 65 or over was $2,897 — almost equivalent to the elderly couple's budget. But the median income of the head only was about $1,900, suggesting that other members of the family contribute quite a bit to the income of older families. Even more important is the fact that a substantial proportion of older families had incomes totaling less than $2,000 in 1960, to say nothing specifically of the "poverty fringe." I therefore believe that the use of average incomes makes the problem look less serious than it is.[14]

[14] For a detailed discussion see Dorothy McCamman, "Low Incomes of the Aged: An Actual Fact or a Statistical Myth?" United States Congress, United States Senate, Special

Table 24. Aggregate Indexes of Economic Insecurity and Security in Old Age

	Ideal	1910	1960	2000
The Insecurity: Old Age				
Frequency: probability at age 14 of reaching 65	100	58	69	?
Severity	0		Gentle upward drift	
The Security: Protection against Old Age*				
Prevention through continued employment	100†	65	30	<25
Alleviation for total aged as a percentage of nondeferrable budget				
Public programs: income as a matter of right	50%	0	38%	50%
Private programs and private means; income as a matter of right	50%	15–20%	22%‡	30–40%
Total	100%	15–20%	60%	80–90%

* These are global data and apply to *all* the aged irrespective of the degree of coverage under public and/or private programs.

† All those who can and want to work.

‡ This increase (over 1910) may appear to be understated. But it should be noted that the large increase in protection developed, for example, under private group programs is yet to be felt, for those so protected are still working.

On the expense side, the elderly couple budget understates for individual cases the problem of medical expense. We shall look at this in detail in the chapter on illness; here note only that a budget of $3,000 can easily swell to $4,000 or $5,000 if a member of the family is sick for a long time. This could also happen, of course, in premature death, but it happens oftener to the elderly, who tend to be at the top of any conventional index of illness.

But the future is perhaps painted gloomier than it is. Though the medical problems of elderly couples still have not been satisfactorily resolved, we are moving much more rapidly toward maintaining their normal income. By 1980 it is expected that all but 9 per cent of those 65 and over will be eligible for OASDI benefits, and in the longer run the coverage figure will rise to 96–98 per cent. Coupled with plans offered by railroads and state and local governments this OASDI coverage will provide a nearly universal floor of protection.[15] Additionally, in 1960

Committee on Aging, *Developments in Aging, 1959 to 1963* (88th Congress, 1st Session), 1963, Appendix D.

[15] Interestingly enough, "universal" coverage or not, universal benefits apparently will not be the rule, if the 1960 experience gave any clue. Social Security Administration press releases in March, 1963, indicated that the Administration was tracking down many peo-

over twenty million people were covered by private pension plans, which will, as they retire, provide additional income. The thickness of the "private carpet" is also improving markedly.

The Rising Price Level

Up to now we have discussed income-maintenance problems while implicitly assuming a stable price level, or mentioned changing prices in passing without speaking of their impact. But old-age annuity contracts (or other forms of old-age income-maintenance programs) customarily provide for payments of fixed amounts during a specified time period; if prices rise, and since 1910 they usually have, the fixed amounts buy less and less every year: purchasing power is eroded.

Between 1910 and 1960, prices approximately tripled — the value of the dollar shrank by two thirds; between 1940 and 1960 prices doubled — the value of the dollar was halved. Longevity is not such that an old person would have lived through the half century from 1910 to 1960, nor would the average old person have lived twenty years from 1940 to 1960. But if we take a decade as a reasonable length for old age, then for every decade from 1910 to 1960 except two (1920–30 and 1930–40) the old person would have found his purchasing power diminished.

Congress has periodically adjusted OASDI benefits to keep them abreast of the cost of living. Other public programs have also been adjusted, though, with some exceptions, to lesser degree; this is true of the federal civil service retirement system and the military retirement system which have recently incorporated automatic cost-of-living features. Some private employers have provided retirement supplements out of pocket, most adjustments being retroactive. In other instances involving group pensions, provision was made for the benefits of future retirements to be adjusted, primarily through the right to purchase additional annuities, or, in collectively bargained plans, through increases in the benefit structure.

Two other solutions to this problem have been brought forward, one of which is in operation, the other as yet only proposed. The first is the variable annuity. Part of the employee's funds are put into equities, on

ple 65 or over who had not applied for their pensions. The reasons for failure to apply are many, but they all add up to the fact that with no change in our economic security system the income maintenance problems of a large number of persons could be improved markedly.

the assumption that equity prices tend to rise with prices in general.[16] Experience with this plan has been brief and limited to a few insurers, but it promises well for the future.

The other solution, still in the proposal stage, envisages constant purchasing power bonds mirroring changes in the consumer price index and thereby effecting an adjustment in purchasing power.[17] As yet the proposal is only an example of man's ingenuity in adjusting to change.

In sum, rising prices over the last half century have increased the income-maintenance problems of the aged; though some accommodation has been made in both public and private programs, the problem is not completely solved, however, and further efforts are needed.

Conclusion

A half century ago there was little difference between the length of a man's working life (measured from normal age at entry into the labor force) and the length of his life. Continuing to work was the primary method of maintaining income for old persons; almost two thirds of those over 65 were in the labor force. For the remaining third few public or private programs maintained income as a matter of the recipients' right, leaving the obligation to be borne principally by relatives and friends, by public assistance based upon need, or by institutions.

In 1960 there was a definite difference between working life and total life, resulting in part from greater longevity, and in part from forced retirement, usually at age 65. Fewer than a third of the aged were in the labor force; maintaining income through working was limited to these. In its place public and private insurance, which maintain income as a matter of right, continued to develop. In 1960 some two thirds of the aged were receiving social insurance benefits; the percentage is growing, and in another several decades it will go over 90 per cent.[18] Under OASDI the average benefit to retired husband and wife was, in 1960,

[16] For a detailed discussion of the variable annuity concept see William C. Greenough, "Pensions — Meeting Price Level Changes," in *Pensions: Problems and Trends*, Homewood, Ill.: Richard D. Irwin, Inc., 1955, pp. 138–60, and Teachers Insurance and Annuity Association, College Retirement Equities Fund, *College Retirement Equities Fund — The First Ten Years of Experience: A Report to Participants*, July, 1962.

[17] For arguments for and against this proposal, see United States Congress, United States Senate, Special Committee on Aging, *A Constant Purchasing Power Bond: A Proposal for Protecting Retirement Income* (87th Congress, 1st Session), 1961.

[18] The percentage eligible will approximate 96–98 per cent, but the percentage receiving social insurance will be smaller.

about $1,500 a year — half of the elderly couple budget. If prices stay relatively stable, this could increase to 76 per cent, given the present maximum OASDI benefit rates. Private pension payments from various sources are currently paid to about 12 per cent of the aged, but this figure should rise considerably in time to come.

A satisfactory public and private system exists at present to provide normal income maintenance for the aged. The problem remaining is essentially that of allocating enough money to meet budgets; this requires increased productivity and economic growth (which is a "real resource" rather than a "money income" problem).

Two problems remain: the aged on the fringes of poverty and the issue of medical expenses. The former we shall touch upon in the final chapter; it might be noted here, however, that as OASDI benefits become more universal, the problem of the aged poor should be minimized. The medical expense question is not so easily answered; it will be the subject of detailed consideration in the chapter on nonoccupational illness.

PREMATURE death, old age, and accidental injury and sickness all lead to economic insecurity through the curtailment of income brought about by unemployment. Though unemployment is the cause in these cases, it differs in an important way from the kind of unemployment we shall talk about in this chapter. In these other kinds of economic insecurity, unemployment results from the inability of the person to work; the cause is internal to the individual. This is most clearly and obviously seen in premature death and disabling illness, but it also may be discerned in old age when productivity falls below some minimum standard.

The kind of unemployment we shall look at here is the kind in which the person is able to work but where no work is available; the cause is external to the individual. People able and willing to work are treated in this chapter; the two preceding and the one to follow dealt with those unable to work or, more rarely, unwilling.[1]

The primary cause of the unemployment dealt with here is economic; that is, the level of economic activity (and of consumer and producer demand) is such that more workers are willing to work at going rates than there are jobs available. This insufficiency of or deficiency in demand may exhibit itself in several ways: it may be general, reaching many different groups, or it may be selective, affecting primarily young workers, or old, or nonwhite, or those in one kind of industry or one part of the country. Usually unemployment contains both general and selective elements; these we shall examine shortly.

Frequency

Before analyzing the frequency of unemployment it will be useful to comment on several problems of measurement, or, more specifically, on conceptual issues behind these measurement problems.

[1] The involuntary unemployment associated with forced retirement — discussed in the last chapter — would fit in here. We chose to treat it earlier because it logically belonged in the discussion of old age.

Premature death and old age are once-and-for-all events. They happen once, they are over with, and there is no returning. In premature death there is no future, and in old age the future is as long as life. Unemployment and accidental injury and sickness are not once-and-for-all events, the chronic cases excepted, but in-and-out events: one loses his job but after a while finds another; one ails but after a while recovers. The chronic cases — the old worker who loses his job and never finds another; the permanently disabled — approach the once-and-for-all, but they are few when compared with all unemployment or all accidental injuries and sicknesses.

Measurement becomes a delicate job in the in-and-out situation. Mortality rates are much less complex. If I said, for example, that the annual mortality rate for a given age group consisting of 100,000 persons was $8\frac{1}{3}$ per cent, it would mean that 8,333 of the 100,000 would die during the time period given. But suppose I say that an annual unemployment rate is $8\frac{1}{3}$ per cent. In the aggregate this means that at any one time $8\frac{1}{3}$ per cent of a population will be jobless. Our approach will not tell us which $8\frac{1}{3}$ per cent any more than the mortality rate would tell who out of the 100,000 would die.

But the mortality rate does tell us that during the year not more than 8,333 persons would die (leaving war and pestilence out of account). Not so for unemployment. One could easily imagine a situation in which each person was unemployed for only thirty days; every month a new group was out of work, and by the end of the year, the entire population could have had thirty days of unemployment.[2] A mortality rate will indicate for some period longer than an instant how many will die; an unemployment rate will tell how many people will be unemployed at a given instant, but not for a longer period, since an annual rate is, for example, only the average of a series of shorter rates.[3] The term unemployment *proportion* has been suggested as more appropriate than unemployment *rate*.

A second difference between premature death on the one hand and unemployment on the other is caused by the relation of the occurrence

[2] A statistically-minded colleague has suggested that what we have in the case of premature death is sampling without replacement, whereas in unemployment it is sampling with replacement. Prediction problems vary between these kinds of insecurity.

[3] Another more specialized counting problem arises in connection with accidental injury and sickness, where the source of data is prevalence surveys. This issue will be considered in the next chapter.

to the environment. Let us put aside the voluntary cases (suicide in premature death; quitting in unemployment) and focus upon the involuntary. We may then say that premature death is more independent of the environment than unemployment is. The environment can be much more readily manipulated to reduce unemployment than it can to reduce premature death: international pressures or large amounts of deficit financing could bring unemployment down as low as it was in World War II; no similar manipulation is possible with premature death.

A third and final measurement issue is definitional. Death is death; in developing rates for it little discretion is required. But is a person unemployed if he has only been indefinitely laid off, or if he is not working because of bad weather, or if he is to report to a new job this week, or if he is working thirty hours rather than forty, or if he is working ten hours? Unemployment is calculated in the United States by a monthly census method,[4] and the census taker must know how to classify each person in his sample.

We are not concerned here with the propriety of the definitions; we know, fortunately, that there has been a consistency of application that permits us to make comparisons over time.[5]

Table 25 pictures unemployment (as an annual average rate) from 1900 through 1962. From this table, we may conclude first that unemployment was lower for the last twenty years of this period than for any other comparable time span, though each new wave of unemployment after 1945 was a little worse than the one before. Second, we conclude that though it is possible to discern a trend, the trend has been most uneven when we take into account the full sixty-year period, by contrast with the trend in premature death.

Unemployment is more than an aggregate phenomenon; it affects individuals in particular walks of life. Specialized data are available back

[4] See *How the Government Measures Unemployment*, United States Department of Labor, May, 1962.

[5] Because of differences in concepts and definitions, there are international differences in application; it has been suggested that if, in the period around 1960, British methods had been used to measure United States unemployment, our rates would have been about half of what United States measures actually indicated. See the *First National City Bank Monthly Letter*, May, 1960, pp. 54–56; Committee for Economic Development Memorandum, *Fiscal and Monetary Policy for High Employment*, 1962, Appendix A, "Unemployment Statistics"; and Joseph S. Zeisel, "Comparison of British and U.S. Unemployment Rates," *Monthly Labor Review*, May, 1962, pp. 489–501.

Table 25. Annual Average Unemployment, 1900–62 (in thousands 14 and over)

Year	Unemployed	% of Civilian Labor Force	Year	Unemployed	% of Civilian Labor Force
1900	1,420	5.0	1931	8,020	15.9
1901	710	2.4	1932	12,060	23.6
1902	800	2.7	1933	12,830	24.9
1903	800	2.6	1934	11,340	21.7
1904	1,490	4.8	1935	10,610	20.1
1905	1,000	3.1	1936	9,030	17.0
1906	280	0.8	1937	7,700	14.3
1907	600	1.8	1938	10,390	19.0
1908	2,960	8.5	1939	9,480	17.2
1909	1,870	5.2	1940	8,120	14.6
1910	2,150	5.9	1941	5,560	9.9
1911	2,290	6.2	1942	2,660	4.7
1912	1,960	5.2	1943	1,070	1.9
1913	1,680	4.4	1944	670	1.2
1914	3,110	8.0	1945	1,040	1.9
1915	3,840	9.7	1946	2,270	3.9
1916	1,920	4.8	1947	2,356	3.9
1917	1,920	4.8	1948	2,325	3.8
1918	560	1.4	1949	3,682	5.9
1919	950	2.3	1950	3,351	5.3
1920	1,670	4.0	1951	2,099	3.3
1921	5,010	11.9	1952	1,932	3.1
1922	3,220	7.6	1953	1,870	2.9
1923	1,380	3.2	1954	3,578	5.6
1924	2,440	5.5	1955	2,904	4.4
1925	1,800	4.0	1956	2,822	4.2
1926	880	1.9	1957	2,936	4.3
1927	1,890	4.1	1958	4,681	6.8
1928	2,080	4.4	1959	3,813	5.5
1929	1,550	3.2	1960	3,913	6.7
1930	4,340	8.9	1961	4,806	5.6
			1962	4,012	5.6

Source: 1900–47, Stanley Lebergott, "Annual Estimates of Unemployment in the United States, 1900–1954," in *The Measurement and Behavior of Unemployment*, Princeton: Princeton University Press, 1957, pp. 215–16; 1947–62, Bureau of the Census. Data from 1957 on are based upon new definitions of unemployment (which add some 200,000 to 300,000 persons); data from 1960 on include Alaska and Hawaii.

Table 26. Characteristics of the Unemployed

Characteristic	% in 1940	% in 1960
Total as percentage of labor force......	14.6%	5.6%
Men		
Under 25	20.9*	11.3
25–44	11.1*	4.3
45 and over	12.4*	4.3
Single	22.3	10.1
Married and living with spouse	11.0	3.0
Widowed or divorced	19.0	7.4
Women		
Under 25	23.9*	10.5
25–44	11.6*	5.5
45 and over	9.2*	3.8
Single	16.0	7.7
Married and living with spouse	6.8	4.7
Widowed or divorced	16.3	4.0
White	15.0	4.3
Nonwhite	18.1	9.5
Agriculture	7.3	8.0
Mining, forestry, fisheries	17.7	9.5
Construction	41.4	12.2
Manufacturing	10.1	6.2
Manufacturing durable goods	9.4	6.3
Manufacturing nondurable goods	10.3	6.0
Transportation and public utilities	8.7	4.3
Wholesale and retail trade	8.1	5.9
Finance, insurance, real estate	5.2	2.4
Service industries	11.1	4.1
Public administration	7.2	2.6
Professional and technical	6.0	1.7
Farmers and farm managers	3.0	0.3
Managers and officials, except farm	2.7	1.4
Clerical	9.2	3.8
Sales	8.9	3.7
Craftsmen	15.1	5.0
Semiskilled workers	12.9	8.0
Domestic workers	10.1	4.9
Service workers	9.7	6.0
Farm laborers	12.5	5.2
Laborers, except farm and mine	33.6	12.5

Source: Bureau of the Census data (1940); *Employment and Earnings*, United States Department of Labor, January, 1961, p. xv.

 * Estimated.

to 1940, though it is not possible to reconstruct the situation as it was a half century ago. The unemployed can be classified by age, sex, color, area, industry, occupation, duration of unemployment, and whether or not a worker was repeatedly unemployed during a given period. Table 26 compares characteristics of the unemployed for 1940 and for mid-1960.[6]

It is no more difficult to tabulate unemployment by geographic area, but it is perhaps less desirable to do so because tabulations tend to be geographical listings of facts more or less readily apparent.[7] High unemployment is associated with declining natural resources, an exodus of industry, particularly severe impacts of recession (as on the automobile industry in Detroit), or shifts in government contract allocations — the last especially significant since 1945.

Persistent unemployment and recurrent unemployment are less obvious in their incidence.[8] Long-term unemployment (15 weeks or more) appears to be associated with certain categories of worker: the older, the nonwhite, the less skilled and less educated, and those from declining occupations, industries, or areas. Moreover, the pervasiveness of long-term unemployment appears to have been on the increase since 1945: in 1948 the average duration of unemployment was 9.8 weeks; by 1960 it had increased to 12.9.

Recurrent unemployment likewise is associated with specific socioeconomic characteristics: one's chances of becoming unemployed more than once in a given period are greater if one is young, is nonwhite, has not completed high school, is an unskilled worker in a service trade, or lives in an area of labor surplus.

We must be careful, however, in interpreting these specialized data;

[6] The interested reader is referred to the following discussions: Philip M. Hauser, "Differential Unemployment and Characteristics of the Unemployed in the United States, 1940–1954," David L. Kaplan, "Unemployment by Industry," and Louis Levine, "Unemployment by Locality and Industry," all in *The Measurement and Behavior of Unemployment*, A Report of the National Bureau of Economic Research, Princeton: Princeton University Press, 1957.

[7] See the monthly publication, *The Labor Market and Employment Security*, United States Department of Labor, Bureau of Employment Security, in which major labor market areas are classified according to relative labor supply.

[8] See Eva Mueller and Jay Schmiedeskamp, *Persistent Unemployment, 1957–1961*, Kalamazoo: W. E. Upjohn Institute for Employment Research, 1962; Jane L. Meredith, "Long-Term Unemployment in the United States," *Monthly Labor Review*, June, 1961, pp. 601–10 plus tables; and the United States Department of Labor study, *Family Characteristics of the Long-Term Unemployed*, of which four parts have been published.

71

the items are interrelated in various ways. For example, the higher unemployment rate for nonwhites is attributable to the fact that the occupations employing the nonwhites are unstable; if such jobs were done by whites, the unemployment rate would be higher for them. It may be suggested, though, that these occupations are the least desirable, and therefore open to nonwhites; which means color is a causal factor after all. With this analysis I should not disagree if the variations are recognized and kept in mind.

Today and Yesterday

Premature death and old age today and fifty years ago are comparable directly and meaningfully for two reasons: the kinds of data are inherently comparable, and comparable methods of collecting data were used during both periods. But for unemployment comparison of the two eras is much harder.

Unemployment data collection using the labor force approach first began in 1940, and has been carried back only as far as 1929 by government agencies. It remained for Stanley Lebergott, working in the fifties, to carry these figures (found in Table 25) back to 1900; only within the last few years have comparable data been developed.

But even with the development of comparable data, a different kind of problem faces the would-be comparer. In premature death and old age there is, year after year, a similarity in the environment within which these phenomena occur. (It may be objected that this is not wholly true: that war and pestilence, or an influenza epidemic, can alter the shape of things. True, but in the United States these are relatively minor exceptions which do not alter the basic trends.) Unemployment is a different breed; there variations are the rule, not the exception. If one uses year-end comparisons, one needs years that are economically like each other for the comparison to have an element of validity. Using Table 25), if one compares 1960 (6.7 per cent unemployment) with 1905 (halfway between 1900 and 1910, and 3.1 per cent unemployment), one must know how similar 1960 and 1905 were; any other comparison needs to be accompanied by detailed study.

Taking this into account, several judgmental conclusions may nevertheless be drawn about comparing yesterday's aggregate unemployment with today's. First, comparisons depend upon the years chosen: if one sets 1960 against 1935 the improvement is apparent; if one compares 1960 with 1906, 1960 does not look so good. But we have learned that unemployment can be controlled, at least in its further reaches. And society has shown an interest in such control: both major political parties are committed to policies that would be unlikely to allow aggregate unemployment to run over 7 or 8 per cent for very long. How far the parties are willing to go to reduce unemployment to such a figure as 3 per cent is much less certain. But one thing is sure: neither party will permit economic deterioration to the point at which the unemployment of the thirties persisted. It seems safe to say that it is not certain whether unemployment in 1970 will be higher or lower than in 1905 or 1925, but it certainly will not be so high as in 1915 or 1935.

Measuring specialized unemployment is well nigh impossible for a number of reasons. For one thing, comparable data go back only to 1940 (with some comparisons possible back to 1930). And, unlike what has been done with aggregate data, no one has sought to carry the record back farther (perhaps an impossible task anyway).

Before 1930, interest was focused upon counting the aggregate unemployed or ascertaining the impact of unemployment rather than upon the composition of the unemployed class and what its characteristics were. We have some data on unemployment by industry and area, but nothing comparable with today's information on age, sex, color, marital status, and occupation.[9] The interest in area and industry statistics appears to have come from a concern to reduce unemployment. Insofar as unemployment was related to cyclical or seasonal instability, such concern was reasonable; finding a remedy required knowing the ailment.

But even if similar data were available, their use for comparative purposes would be questionable because of basic changes in the nature and structure of the economy between 1900–10 and 1950–60. Broad comparisons can be made, but comparison at specific points is harder. For example: To say area A had high unemployment in 1910 and area B in 1960 tells us little unless we also know what happened to these areas during the intervening years. Or to say that older people currently are highly unemployed but that they were not in 1900 explains nothing unless we find what underlying changes have taken place.

The following conjectures contrast, for a given level of aggregate un-

---

[9] Some works on earlier studies are Paul H. Douglas and Aaron Director, *The Problem of Unemployment*, New York: Macmillan, 1931, Part One, and *Bibliography of Unemployment*, Geneva: International Labour Office, 1930.

employment, particular aspects of unemployment in 1960 and in 1900. Unemployment among older workers is higher today because industrial technology has moved in a way prejudicial to the elderly, despite seniority clauses that afford a degree of protection to the older worker. Unemployment among workers under 25 is higher today because fewer youths are remaining on farms, where employment was "automatic." Unemployment of the nonwhite is higher today because the kinds of job nonwhites increasingly have come to hold are those inherently less stable. Unemployment among women today is lower; though it is true that females have increased proportionately in the labor force, they have entered relatively more stable occupations. Moreover, with relatively low levels of unemployment, the lump-of-labor pressure is not exerted upon them as it is at higher levels.

Unemployment rates for the widowed and divorced are higher today because there are relatively more of them in the aggregate. Though we have no direct comparative data, high school dropouts, the unskilled, and minority groups form a disproportionately large part of the unemployed — a larger part than they did fifty years ago. The testimony of the Secretaries of Labor, 1960–62, suggests that each of these groups suffers not a 6 but a 12 per cent unemployment rate. Industrially or occupationally there have been no marked shifts; the unstable categories of yesteryear are not much more stable today; for example, consumer goods are more stable today than producer goods — as they also were yesterday.

But some important facts need further examination.

Structural Unemployment

A controversy that has drawn considerable attention in the past several years centers on whether higher unemployment levels (since 1955–57) are a consequence of "structural" changes in the composition of the labor force, or of weakness in aggregate demand. The answer is important because the two situations call for two different kinds of remedy.[10]

[10] For a discussion of the problems and the conclusions see Council of Economic Advisers, *The American Economy in 1961: Problems and Policies*, Supplement B; United States Congress, Joint Economic Committee, Subcommittee on Economic Statistics, *Employment and Unemployment* (87th Congress, 2nd Session), 1962; United States Congress, Joint Economic Committee, Subcommittee on Economic Statistics, *Higher Unemployment Rates, 1957–1960: Structural Transformation or Inadequate Demand?* (87th Congress, 1st Session), 1961.

All the evidence is not yet in, nor are all the conclusions clear. The trend appears, however, to be in the following directions. "The major problem is inadequate total demand, but the situation has been aggravated by some serious structural problems: immobility of labor and capital; workers without the training and experience for new job opportunities opening up in our economy; particular local areas in which, for one reason or the other, dynamic changes in technology and demand have left resources without profitable employment." [11]

In its purest form the structural unemployment thesis assumes that the total number of job opportunities is adequate, but that the process by which displaced workers move into new jobs has become longer and hence the "float" of the unemployed has increased. Structural unemployment may thus be regarded as an extreme form of frictional unemployment. The remedy proposed is not the creation of more jobs but the facilitation of the movement of the unemployed into existing jobs.[12]

Adjustments to counteract structural imbalance are less costly today than they were twenty-five or fifty years ago, and the costs of moving plants and/or workers are lower today, relative to income. Moreover, today most skilled jobs have more of a common core of skills, teaching techniques are better, and training programs can be devised to permit shifts formerly not feasible. If the structural problem is, in fact, less serious than it was some years ago, the skeptic may ask why there has been a sudden increase in public and private retraining and redevelopment programs. The answer appears to lie in changed social goals: we are no longer willing to tolerate the degree of unemployment caused by the structural problem. Then too, since the mid-1950's a gap has widened between potential and actual gross national product; reducing resource unemployment would help close that gap. A generation ago society would more readily have tolerated it.

[11] *1963 Joint Economic Report* (Report No. 78), United States Congress, United States Senate (88th Congress, 1st Session), 1963, p. 4.

[12] Research on both supply and demand aspects of the problem has been undertaken (1961–62) by the Council of Economic Advisers under Chairman Walter W. Heller. The previously cited *The American Economy in 1961: Problems and Policies*, Supplement B, statistically indicates that on the supply side the increase in unemployment since 1955–57 has been across the board and not concentrated structurally. On the demand side, an analysis of help wanted ads as a manifestation of vacancies and therefore of labor demand shows both an unadjusted and an adjusted *decline* between 1955–57 and 1962. See the previously cited *Higher Unemployment Rates, 1957–60*, pp. 23, 73–74.

75

Index of Unemployment: Today and Yesterday

In comparing my chances of premature death or longevity with those of my father and grandfather, a common factor, age, permitted direct quantitative comparison. This is not true of unemployment, where the variables are numerous enough to make difficult if not rule out a direct comparison. But if we assume the same profession and age for all three of us, the probabilities might run as follows for a given time: chances of unemployment in the 1950's, about 1 in 20; chances of unemployment in the 1930's, about 1 in 5; chances of unemployment in the 1900's, about 1 in 25. That is, 1901–10 would have been the best period, 1931–40 the worst.

As for the influence of particular variables upon unemployment, the picture might be as shown in the accompanying tabulation, which compares the 1960 with the 1900 chances of unemployment's befalling various kinds of worker. Even if this picture is of only very general accuracy

Worker's Characteristic	Chance of Unemployment in 1960
Older (45–50 or over)	Greater
Younger (under 21)	Greater
Nonwhite	Greater
High school dropout	Greater
Female (any age)	Probably less
Divorced, separated, widow, widower	Greater
Skilled (25–45)	Less
In consumer goods industry	Probably little change
In producer goods industry	Probably little change
In depressed area	Probably little change except for location of area

it points up two major trends: first, the increase in the skill required for jobs, the difficulties of the unskilled, and the need to reduce obstacles, such as dropping out of high school, to the acquisition of skills; and second, discrimination in the labor market affecting nonwhites, older people, and other groups.[13]

Having every willing worker working is hardly a conceivable ideal; achieving it would mean a rigidity the economy could not allow. But full employment, properly defined, is the goal.

Most broadly, full employment can be regarded as an economic as

[13] Though it might be contended that not hiring the unskilled is also discrimination, it is not so if the job calls for skill. But not hiring the nonwhite or the older person may be discriminatory, for they might well be able to do the job. The nub of the argument is that the unskilled person cannot do the job; the nonwhite or older person may be able to.

well as a political and social policy. But to be more useful the term needs more precision, which may be brought about by applying a statistical series and selecting cutoff points in that series. In the United States the definition most commonly used is minimum total unemployment, and the series used to measure that total unemployment is the aforementioned *Monthly Report on the Labor Force.*

In this statistical series, which measures unemployment as a percentage of the labor force, the percentage of unemployment that can be allowed under "full" employment can hardly be zero, for this would mean an undesirably rigid economy. The current consensus appears to regard 4 per cent as a desirable intermediate minimum unemployment. Reaching this goal would mean reducing unemployment from the 6 per cent levels of the early 1960's. In the long run, the current consensus is that a level between 2 and 3 per cent might eventually be reached; many people would apparently settle for 3 per cent.

We do not know why we are not doing better — why, instead of 6 per cent, we have not reached 4 per cent, or 3 per cent unemployment. We do know that our growth rate is not so high as it could be, with the result that the slack in unemployment has not been taken up. Raising the level of growth has been of primary concern to economists and politicians in the 1960's, and in the early 1960's several conclusions emerged. In the last twenty or more years we have been able to keep unemployment below 8 per cent, and, for about half that period, below 4. The period from 1940 to 1950 was better than that from 1950 on, and each succeeding post–World War II recession has driven unemployment up a little higher than before. Whether the relatively good record since 1940 is a result of economic circumstances or of judicious governmental direction is for the reader to decide, but there is little doubt that we have economic knowledge today that would permit us, through monetary, fiscal, and other policies, to hold unemployment well below the frightening levels of the 1930's. The closer we get to our goal, however, even if it is only 4 per cent unemployment, the more difficult it becomes to get even closer to it, for two reasons: though we have little doubt about the good that comes from applying great doses of money, we are much less certain about the effectiveness of applying them at the margin; and as we approach full employment undesirable side effects like inflation may become more likely. That is, we are not only uncertain about the policies to pursue as we come closer to full employment, but we are also concerned over undesirable consequences. One might therefore predict that though it is very unlikely that we shall witness anything like the unemployment levels of the thirties, we may not get down to 4 per cent or below for any protracted period of years.

The Alleviative Ideal and Current Reality

To return to what may by now appear to be a truism: it is not realistic to expect one hundred per cent success in preventing economic insecurity, no matter what might be hypothetically possible. Since the economically insecure (here the unemployed) are an overhead cost to society, the question again becomes how and in what degree to provide income maintenance or restoration.

Let us take the problem of degree first. In premature death and old age we suggested the ideal of permitting the family to live as it had previously. In both these cases the duration of the insecurity is long — in old age until death, in premature death until there is a basic change in circumstances, remarriage or old age.

But unemployment, except for chronic cases, is of short duration. In 1961, for example, 40 per cent of the jobless were unemployed for less than five weeks, and, cumulatively, 70 per cent were unemployed for less than fifteen weeks. This difference in duration suggests a difference in the level of income maintenance: Over the long run, all normal budget costs become nondeferrable, but in the short run, certain costs can be deferred. Hence, for unemployment, a first approximation of a protective ideal might be maintaining income to meet nondeferrable expenses, a concept introduced above (pp. 30–31) with the nondeferrable budget.

This approximation needs additional examination, because economic unemployment is in certain respects fundamentally different from premature death and old age. We have said that both premature death and old age cause long-run problems; technically, then, no expenditure can be deferred; things can be foregone — the automobile never purchased, the trip never taken — but expenditures cannot be postponed indefinitely. In the long run the deferrable becomes the nondeferrable, or it really is not a cost; moreover, by that time we are all dead, as a famous economist commented.[14]

[14] We are using expenditure as the equivalent of explicit monetary outlay, thus avoiding the term cost. If households kept books in a technical accounting sense, all costs would

In the short run one might suggest that purchases of capital items, items whose consumption life is of extended duration, are deferrable. The dress can be worn longer, the automobile will run for another thousand miles, the refrigerator will continue to run for a while. Repair charges may arise, and they are legitimately nondeferrable.

Nondeferrable expenditures are those associated with goods whose consumption life is short; food is the prime example. For us, such contractual obligations as the payment on the house and the life insurance premium may also be nondeferrable.[15]

The net effect of deferrability is to reduce the need and the budget of the unemployed. The longer the unemployment, the lower the deferrability; in permanent unemployment one thus reaches the long duration of premature death or old age. The degree of budgetary reduction possible is a matter we shall look at shortly.

The unemployed, through foresight and saving, can, more easily than those afflicted with old age or premature death, meet some of their nondeferrable expenses, because unemployment is short run.

To recapitulate: An ideal level of protection against economic insecurity would be maintaining income to meet an adequate budget, less for the short run than for the long, because during a short period certain expenditures are deferrable. Because unemployment is short run, its income maintenance problems are lower than those for premature death or old age. In addition, the level of protection provided by government might be lower in the short run, with more individual responsibility. The government's floor of protection might be 50 per cent of the nondeferrable budget or approximately 67 per cent of the city worker's normal budget.

Perhaps the most important influence, not on the level of protection as such but rather on the amount of that protection provided by outside sources such as government, is incentive. The problem is whether people whose income is maintained while they are idle (unemployed)

go on, though for some, such as depreciation on the family automobile, no explicit monetary payment to others would be made. Since households do not operate this way, we tailor our discussion to how they do behave, irrespective of what the niceties of accounting or economics might call for.

[15] This class of expenditure can become elusive and slippery: one must have shelter, and either payments on a house are being made or rent is being paid. But is insurance a necessity? Moreover, some contractual obligations may be deferrable; one merchandising organization has proposed that debts owed it for purchases made on time be held in abeyance while a debtor is unemployed.

will have any incentive to go back to work. This problem does not arise in premature death: the deceased cannot choose to return to work. Similarly in old age: the old person is deliberately cut out of the labor force.[16] But the unemployed have two choices, at least in theory: income from work or substitute income. These choices may sometimes not be possible; income maintenance systems are policed to keep workers from receiving substitute income when work is available.

But — to repeat this major point — it is likely that the closer income maintenance programs come to paying the same amount as the last job, the greater the incentive problem will be. It follows that external income maintenance programs should meet only part of the budget, thus encouraging the unemployed person to go back to work if possible.[17]

A budget for the unemployed worker and his family may be based on the city worker's family budget presented above (p. 30), where we used an average annual figure of $6,200. I recognize that average unemployment may last for perhaps only a fourth of a year, but for comparative purposes it is better to stay on an annual basis.

We cannot, first of all, decrease the budget as we could in the premature death case; but not working does lower such work expenses as the cost of transportation by an amount we shall estimate at $100, leaving a budget of $6,100.[18] Some analysts have suggested that these working expenses are just about counterbalanced by the fringe benefits foregone when not working; I agree, but we are concerned here only with outflow and cannot balance these off against each other.

Admitting wide individual variations, we deducted as deferrable parts of the following components of the city worker's budget: food away from home, house furnishings, clothing, automobile, recreation, and gifts and contributions,[19] or $1,200, which leaves a budget of $4,900.

[16] One can think of minor or noneconomic problems: excessive income maintenance for a widow might prevent her making desirable readjustments, or high retirement income might pull people out of the labor force too soon.

[17] If self-policing were perfect, this problem would not exist, and if external policing were perfect, the problem could be controlled. But policing increases markedly as wage restoration rises, and a lower degree of restoration is really a substitute for other administrative control.

[18] All our judgments are based upon the original budget data in "The City Worker's Budget," *Monthly Labor Review*, August, 1960, pp. 785–808.

[19] We obviously made value judgments here. We did not regard all the clothing component as deferrable (given a wife and two children in this family); we instead assumed that two fifths of the total clothing budget was deferrable. Nor did we expect the family to stop smoking or drinking, allowances for both of which are found in the budget.

Taxes (at least part), including OASDI taxes, remain to be deducted, and this deduction is legitimate because under the law income from such sources as unemployment compensation is nontaxable. Subtracting an estimated $700 for taxes, we have $4,200 for a family of four, as compared with $4,500 for a family of three in the premature death case (p. 31). The basic difference is in the nondeferrable expenses, assumed to be greater in premature death. It is interesting to note a kind of common denominator in the three budgets we have looked at so far: around 1960 the adequate minimum budget in the United States averaged $1,500 per person. This glosses over various kinds of indivisibility problems — the cost of housing for a couple may be nowhere near double that for a single person. But the common denominator is there.

In the second and third chapters we saw budgets for about 1910 ranging from a high of $850 (northern cities, 1913) to a low of $600 (southern cities, about 1911). In reducing such budgets to the nondeferrable expense level we note immediately that the degree of reduction is much less than would be possible fifty years later for two reasons: though taxes were nonexistent in these early budgets, in 1960 they were some 10 per cent; and insofar as the larger capital expenditures of 1960 could be postponed the budget could be reduced more readily.

For 1960, we reduced the budget by 30 per cent, from $6,100 to $4,200. In the 1910–15 budgets it appeared that clothing and amusement were the only areas for reduction. If we cut amusement entirely from one budget ($20 out of $649) and reduced clothing by 50 per cent ($120 to $60), we would have a net reduction of $80 on a $649 budget, or approximately 12 per cent. This may be slightly high; a rounded figure of 10 per cent might not be unjust. But whichever budget one selects ($600 low, $850 high), a 10 per cent decrease is about the most one could expect to lower expenses to a nondeferrable level, leaving budgets of $540 and $765 respectively, which we shall use here and in the next chapter.

In the last two chapters we gave good marks, qualitatively and relatively, to society's efforts to counteract the insecurities of premature death and old age, but the effort to solve the problems of unemployment has been less complete. Except for medical care, no problem has had less successful treatment. Public programs in this area are both narrower in coverage and lesser in the degree of income restoration than are their counterparts in the death and old-age fields. For a variety of reasons, many of them actuarial, private programs do not exist, except for the relatively small supplementary unemployment benefit plans and various informal approaches; thus there is no real counterpart to the private insurance and annuities that cover death and old age.

These differences have several causes, two of which I shall mention. The principal public program, unemployment insurance (or compensation), is a combined federal-state program that gives the states considerable judgment, as, for example, in setting benefit levels, whereas OASDI is a wholly federal program. Were unemployment insurance a federal program the income maintenance achievements would be greater (if all the states' rights problems could be solved). On the private program side, unemployment is not responsive to the insurance approach; thus no real alternatives exist as they do for death and old age.

We have said (pp. 30–31) that the premature death family's budget was $4,500, that average income restoration was about $3,000, or 66⅔ per cent, and that this kind of protection was currently almost universal. The old-age budget was $3,000, with 1960 average income restoration about $1,500, or 50 per cent; present coverage is over 70 per cent, and growing so that perhaps after 1980 some 95 per cent of those reaching 65 will be eligible for benefits.

But in 1960 only about 60 per cent of the unemployed were eligible for benefits, and only 45 to 50 per cent of them receiving benefits. This suggests that unemployment was higher among the uninsured than the insured or that part of the currently uninsured had exhausted their benefits. I shall use the 50 per cent figure rather than the 45 for ease of calculation.

The unemployed family budget was $4,200 (pp. 80–81). A rule of thumb used since the passage of the Social Security Act in 1935 is that unemployment insurance should restore half to two thirds of lost wages. Two thirds of the $4,200 (which we shall substitute for lost wages) is $2,800. If the 1960 average weekly payment for total unemployment of $32.87 were paid for fifty-two weeks (though the common maximum is twenty-six), the income would have been about $1,700, 40 per cent of the $4,200.[20] Technically, any short-run income restoration figure we

[20] This is calculated on the unemployed family budget base. Interestingly enough, a series of studies made in the period 1958–60 showed benefits averaging 38–42 per cent of the *previous wages* of covered persons. Again we do an injustice to reality through using averages — in this case an average family. Many unemployed families may be larger than average or have two unemployed members. And some of the unemployed are young, single persons living at home.

arrive at should be modified by allowing for the waiting period, customarily one week, specified in almost all state laws.

We may now say that in 1960, 50 per cent of the economically unemployed were getting unemployment compensation, on the average about 40 per cent of their budgets. The accompanying tabulation sets this forth. Thus, instead of being required (on an annual basis) to provide

	Suggested	*Actual (1960)*
Nondeferrable income restored by UI	67%	40%
Balance to be met by private means	33%	60%

$1,400, or a third of the annual budget, the economically unemployed in this group had to provide $2,500, or 60 per cent. Again it should be said that with common maximum benefit periods of 26 weeks the above example would be more realistic had we based it on a half year.

In addition to whatever individual private means the unemployed may have, one or both of two group income maintenance plans may be available to certain members; dismissal compensation or severance pay programs and supplementary unemployment benefit plans. There are also somewhat specialized, but important and growing, plans, in meat-packing and longshoring, designed to provide security in unemployment caused by automation or other similar economic challenges.

Dismissal compensation is a specified amount paid, in addition to back pay or salary, by an employer to an employee when the employment is permanently ended for reasons beyond the employee's control. Some current plans provide for payment in temporary layoffs, but most as yet do not. Thus if a separated employee can get severance pay in addition to unemployment benefits, he has a means of increasing his level of income. In 1960 eighteen states restricted unemployment benefits when dismissal payments were being received, seven totally disqualifying the person and eleven allowing the payment of the difference, if any, between the unemployment benefit and the severance pay; the other states had no such restrictions. In 1960 some six to eight million employees were covered by such plans.[21] If unemployment were distributed among these employees in the same ratio as in the population at large, and if we take into account the incidence of temporary versus permanent separation as well as state limitations on concurrent receipt

---

[21] From my "Memorandum on Unemployment Insurance in the United States," unpublished, prepared for the Committee for Economic Development, 1960.

of benefits, we might say that two per cent of our first group (one per cent of the total unemployed) were receiving income sufficient to reach the 67 per cent restoration level.

Supplementary unemployment benefits covering an estimated two million employees were introduced in the historic automobile negotiations in 1955. Though there are variations, the basic plan is this: [22] A base rate is first selected — 65 per cent of weekly after-tax straight-time pay, for example — and the unemployment insurance benefit the person is eligible for is subtracted from this amount. The balance is then made up by the supplementary unemployment benefits payment, subject to a weekly maximum, such as $25 or $40. The payment may be made for twenty-six weeks, or fifty-two, as is increasingly common.

In 1960 about $100 million were paid out in supplementary unemployment benefits (compared with $3.02 billion in benefits under all types of public unemployment insurance programs). Unemployment rates for those eligible for supplementary unemployment benefits appear to have been about half those for the whole labor force. Applying this factor to our categories we may conclude that another three per cent of our first group (one and a half per cent of the total unemployed) had income sufficient to put them at the 67 per cent restoration level.

It is also likely that some people, through various formal and informal programs, had their entire income restored during the period in question (though if unemployment lasted long enough this would cease to be true). These people are most likely to be serving in managerial positions or similar capacities or covered by some special severance-pay plan — a baseball manager or a football coach whose contracts have been bought up, for example. I believe, however, that this group is very small, a fraction of one per cent, and it is therefore not feasible to work it into the totals.

To summarize: of the 1960 currently unemployed five per cent were being paid through unemployment insurance and severance pay or supplementary unemployment benefits, 67 per cent of their deferred expense budget; forty-five per cent were being paid, from unemployment insurance only, 40 per cent; and fifty per cent had no help from either of these sources.

In the second chapter we estimated that net equity per married couple was $4,300 in 1960. If all this were liquid, it would provide a

[22] For details see Turnbull, Williams, and Cheit, *op. cit.*, p. 53.

sum sufficient to meet the budgetary shortages for the first two groups in the summary paragraph above, assuming in both cases that unemployment lasted a year (since for a shorter period the liquid net equity would obviously cover all the shortages), and also provide $4,300 or full income maintenance for the group with no formal public or private maintenance.

Here is where our averages really break down. Even if we assume that the median and the mean net equity are the same, recurrent unemployment makes impossible such a use of net equity because it has been partly or entirely used up. Equity is not something automatically replenished quarterly or annually; it takes time to save. Moreover, it is likely that the median is actually lower than the mean — and far lower for that important group of unemployed in the poverty group we shall speak of in the last chapter. Table 27 provides some information on how the insured unemployed bridge the gap between unemployment benefits and budgetary needs. There were differences from one study to another in the description of the period to which these data refer. For example, in the report published for the St. Louis study, all these adjustments purportedly refer to the whole survey year; whereas in the report on the Tampa–St. Petersburg study, the data are all listed as adjustments made during unemployment. Because of the nature of the information requested of claimants, however, and because the questionnaire form used was the same in each study, it is reasonable to expect that the reported adjustments for the most part represent changes made by households as a result of the unemployment of claimants interviewed. Hence the data are useful and allow broad comparison from one study to another.

Another set of government studies sheds some light on what happens after benefits have been exhausted.[23] A calculation of averages from these studies suggests the following. Within two months after exhaustion 30 per cent were re-employed (the range in the various states was from 13 to 41 per cent), 10 per cent dropped out of the labor force (the range was from 4 to 18 per cent), and 60 per cent were still unemployed (the range was from 51 to 71 per cent). Within four months after exhaustion 40 per cent were re-employed (the range was from 16 to 53 per

[23] *Experience of Claimants Exhausting Benefit Rights under Unemployment Insurance, 17 Selected States,* United States Department of Labor, Bureau of Employment Security (BES No. U-178), December, 1958, and a similar study (mimeographed report for 16 states, 1956–59) issued by the Bureau of Employment Security in April, 1961.

Table 27. Economic Adjustments Made by Claimants' Households during Claimants' Unemployment

| | Used Savings | | | | | | Received | | | | | |
Type of Claimant	Had Savings	Ex-hausted Savings	Cashed Securities	Increased Debts to Stores	Bor-rowed	Friends' or Rela-tives' Help	Free Medical or Dental Help	Relief Goods and Services	Cash Relief	Dropped Life Insur-ance	Post-poned Medical or Dental Care	Post-poned Buying House or Durable Goods
Pittsburgh, Pa.												
Single†	45%	18%	7%		20%		7%	12%		35%		
In 4-person household												
Head†	42	14	15		46		12	27		33		
Tampa–St. Petersburg, Fla.												
Single	50	16	12		17		12	18		11	17	20
In 4-person household												
Head	22	6	2		25		7	2		5	24	16
Nonhead	2	0	3		28		3	2		2	20	17
Anderson–Greenville–Spartanburg, S.C.												
Single	18	8	10	29	8	20	0	0	0	16	20	31
In 4-person household												
Head	14	12	4	45	33	31	9	6	2	8	33	40
Nonhead	10	6	15	53	33	9	4	0	0	6	23	45

Table 27. Continued

| Type of Claimant | Used Savings | | Cashed Securities | Increased Debts to Stores | Borrowed | Friends' or Relatives' Help | Received | | | Dropped Life Insurance | Postponed Medical or Dental Care | Postponed Buying House or Durable Goods |
	Had Savings	Exhausted Savings					Free Medical or Dental Help	Relief Goods and Services	Cash Relief			
Albany-Schenectady-Troy, N.Y.												
Single	25	2	5	31	8	8	0	3	0	0	22	18
In 4-person household												
Head	34	5	11	54	11	31	17	9	5	6	40	31
Nonhead	30	2	9	43	11	5	9	2	0	1	27	25
Portland, Ore.												
Single	33	5	4	26	15	12	4	2	2	9	22	29
In 4-person household												
Head	37	9	7	50	35	22	5	3	4	11	48	54
Nonhead	34	3	8	47	46	16	4	3	5	9	39	49
St. Louis, Mo.‡												
Single	54	10	35		5	20	3	1	0	4	28	11
In 4-person household												
Head	75	10	33	16	16	35	19	7	4	6	41	9
Nonhead	51	4	46	11	11	10	7	1	5	3	31	10

Source: Bureau of Employment Security, United States Department of Labor.

* Individual items do not necessarily add up to 100 per cent since some households made more than one adjustment and others none.

† Includes claimants with 1 to 6 weeks of unemployment at the time of the survey.

‡ Percentages are based on number of claimants in a position to make particular adjustments (e.g., number who decreased savings is compared only with those who had savings) . By contrast, the percentages in each of the other cities are based on all claimants in the study.

cent), 13 per cent dropped out of the labor force (the range was from 7 to 20 per cent), and 47 per cent were still unemployed (the range was from 35 to 73 per cent). The most common reasons for leaving the labor force after exhaustion are retirement and illness (males) and household responsibilities (females). Exhaustion claimants used the following means of support: 35–40 per cent reported help from spouse or immediate family, 12–15 per cent did odd jobs, 30–35 per cent used savings or borrowed, 2–3 per cent reported they went on public relief.

With the case of the person with no benefits to exhaust, who is not covered by unemployment insurance, we pass from the factual realm of social statistics (incomplete though they be) to the fictional world of John Steinbeck. In a very real sense fiction is the better source of information here, because of the lack of social statistics. The insured unemployed who exhaust their benefits eventually fall into this noninsured category, but at least while they were drawing benefits they are identifiable. Those never insured are anonymous, unknown, and it is hard to get information about them. For one thing, there is no easy way to identify them. Though the insured unemployed are identified by their use of the unemployment compensation system, the uninsured are not.[24] And if the uninsured unemployed cannot be identified, there is no way of getting data from them (even if they could be identified, the cost of getting would be very high). Finally, if they are identified, as when they apply for relief, this is a local and state matter, and national summations are apparently not compiled for these cases.

Piecing together such information as could be got, however, we get the following picture of uninsured unemployed. On an annual average there were between one and two million of them a year about 1960. This is a net figure for those who exhaust their benefits and drift into the uninsured. They are uninsured because of not being in covered employment, or because, if they were in covered employment, they were not eligible or they exhausted their benefits. I believe that they tend to be more marginal as employees than are the insured unemployed. This compounds the problem, for the likelihood of their returning soon to work is less, and the likelihood of their having accumulated resources to tide them over is also less. To keep body and soul together they run

[24] Through cross-checking between the *Monthly Report on the Labor Force* and *The Insured Unemployed* some identification might be made, but it would be aggregative and a halting first step.

through their own resources and then through friends and relatives, private help, and general assistance (public relief), which is the residual program in the United States.

Categorical programs such as those of the federal-state grant-in-aid variety offer some means of support — old-age assistance, aid to dependent children (for which a special fourteen-month program permitting the extension of help to the children of the unemployed was intro-

Table 28. Indexes of Economic Insecurity and Security in Unemployment

	Ideal	1900	1910	1930	1950	1960
The Insecurity: Unemployment						
Frequency: Aggregate chance of unemployment	2.5%	5%	6%	9%	7%	
Severity: chance of prolonged unemployment, need to relocate in other types of work.	?		Gently rising to 1930, followed by steep increases, descent in 1940's, and increase again after 1950.			
*The Security: Explicit Income Protection against Unemployment**						
Public programs: unemployment insurance						
For unemployed population as a whole	67%		0	0		20%
For segment of unemployed currently eligible for such insurance	67%		0	0		40%
Private group programs: severance pay, SUB						
For unemployed population as a whole	?					2½%
For segment of unemployed eligible for such benefits....	?					5%
Subtotal, excluding private means, unemployed population as a whole....	67%					25%
Private personal means permitting income maintenance						
Average population as a whole	33%		40%	45%		100%
Adjusted to unemployed population: their use of assets, chances for asset accumulation	10%		13%	15%		20%
Total alleviative income restoration	100%		13%	15%		40–45%

* Percentage of income restoration of nondeferrable expense budget, explicitly payable or available, and obtainable as a matter of right.

duced on May 8, 1961, and was later extended to June 30, 1967), aid to the blind, and aid to the permanently and totally disabled. Likewise the disability benefits of OASDI afford a basis of help. But these are sharply limited to cases of unemployment where the whole person changes status. The distribution of surplus food also helps; in 1961 some $140 million worth of such commodities were donated.

General assistance is the most common form of public income maintenance program for the uninsured unemployed, though not always, for some jurisdictions deny relief to the employable. As recently as fifteen years ago eighteen states denied in one way or another aid to the employable.[25] Though this situation has improved, restrictions remain. General assistance payments, aggregated for the United States, were $444 million in 1940, dropped to below $300 million in 1950–57, and then began a climb which reached a high of $466 million in 1961. Of course there is no way of identifying what part of the total went to the unemployed, but some must have.

A half century ago there were no public unemployment insurance programs, nor were there severance pay or supplementary unemployment benefit programs as we know them, although a handful of severance pay plans did exist, and a few union and/or employer unemployment plans. The unemployed of the time had to depend upon their own resources, the help of friends and relatives, private charity, and, as a last resort, public assistance of some kind. Another kind of adjustment which no longer takes place was also made in those earlier days: immigrants returned to Europe during periods of high unemployment in the United States.

Table 28 compares insecurity in 1960 and in 1910.

Policy Comments and Proposals

If we apply the twin criteria of the extent of coverage under economic security programs and the level of income restoration, then society has accommodated much less successfully to economic unemployment than to either premature death or old age, for several possible reasons.

Insofar as a floor of protection is provided at all it is provided by the state government in the case of unemployment. Though there are federal standards (which do not, however, include benefit standards) in-

---

[25] See Eveline M. Burns, *The American Social Security System*, Boston: Houghton Mifflin, 1951, p. 345.

corporated in the Social Security Act of 1935 — standards the states are not free to undercut in their own unemployment insurance laws — federal action has done little or nothing to improve this economic security law. The impetus for improvement must therefore come from the states; though some progress has been made, it has been smaller than in OASDI. States hesitate to move too fast; unemployment insurance taxes business enterprises, and a state may believe that if it gets out of line it may create a climate unfavorable to new firms and discouraging to existing ones. Unified federal control and action would make change much less difficult.

Old age and premature death pose few if any incentive problems; economic unemployment does. How real and how important quantitatively and qualitatively these incentive and other abuse problems are has been analyzed elsewhere.[26] At the state level there is apparently enough legislative concern to prevent the degree of improvement found in several other economic security programs. In the private sector, there is for the hazard of unemployment no counterpart for life insurance in premature death and the annuity in old age. The lack of such insurance means that the person who wants to protect himself must do it himself, not by pooling risks.

In premature death and old age we saw that preventively, except for the employment problems of the old, society seems to be responding in a positive way to the insecurities. Alleviatively, we saw that both the floor of protection and its covering were being provided satisfactorily, and that the basic problem is economic growth to provide additional resources for those facing these insecurities.

In economic unemployment things are different. Preventively a better job can be done, whether through monetary and fiscal policy or through direct, special programs focusing on the under-25 group, the nonwhites, the technologically displaced or through some combination of these approaches remains to be seen. We need research, analysis, and experiment; we are not likely to get far by passively sitting on our hands.[27]

Similarly in the area of alleviation. In unemployment insurance, the

[26] See, for example, Joseph M. Becker, *The Problem of Abuse in Unemployment Benefits — A Study of Limits*, New York: Columbia University Press, 1955.

[27] See John T. Dunlop, "Public Policy and Unemployment," United States Congress, United States Senate, Special Committee on Unemployment Problems, *Studies in Unemployment* (86th Congress, 2nd Session), 1960.

floor of protection and indeed much of the covering must be provided by the public program of unemployment insurance, which at present covers only 60 or so per cent of the labor force, leaving a gaping hole. All groups — the self-employed, for example — cannot be readily covered by the system, but I suggest that more than thirteen million wage and salary earners could be, increasing coverage 78 per cent.[28]

Benefits should be increased to come closer to the 50 to 67 per cent income restoration level envisaged in this law, rather than the approximately 40 per cent present restoration. It would, moreover, be desirable to provide a mechanism (already at work in a few states) to allow benefits to be adjusted to changing wage levels. Whether benefits should be extended automatically as a recession worsens may be debated; I think they should.

Financing proposals would include the possible increase of the tax base from $3,000 to $4,800 (to build greater stability into the system),[29] and rate structures that combine a base rate (which all employers would pay) with an experience rating component (which would vary with the employer's own record).

Improvement is not a one-way street. Qualifications for benefits need review; in 1960 about a fifth of the states had the same wage qualifications as they did in 1950, even though wages had risen appreciably.[30]

In the present federal-state framework, the best that can be done is to exhort the states to improve. If one believes that this leads only to piecemeal and inadequate improvement, one can suggest, as is suggested here, additional federal standards — an increase in the minimum specifications in the federal law.

In the public sector there is also a need to improve the general assistance program, possibly through federal grants-in-aid, to maintain income for the uninsured unemployed (or for those who exhaust their benefits) and to prevent erosion of the unemployment insurance system — to keep it from becoming a general dole.

[28] On this and other points see United States Congress, United States Senate, Special Committee on Unemployment Problems, *Report of the Special Committee* (86th Congress, 2nd Session, Report No. 1206), 1960.

[29] Another suggestion would be to make the unemployment insurance base the same as OASDI's.

[30] For more proposals see R. A. Lester, *The Economics of Unemployment Compensation*, Princeton University, Industrial Relations Section, 1962, Ch. 9, and *Unemployment Insurance Legislative Policy, Recommendations for State Legislation, 1962*, United States Department of Labor, Bureau of Employment Security (BES No. U-212), 1962.

Unemployment insurance is not well suited to the income maintenance problems of the young entrant into the labor force, the technologically displaced, the long-term unemployed. Nor is general assistance
(relief) well-suited in and of itself as a mechanism to get people back
into productive activity. We require programs that improve the operation of the employment service, that facilitate area redevelopment,
that retrain, that respond to automation.[31] We should not optimistically
expect that the governmental bureaucracy will resolve all these problems, but they are problems it must tackle.

In the private sector businesses should plan in advance as much as
possible to minimize the displacement of employees. There are limits
to this, obviously; there are also possibilities as yet untapped. No conditions should be put upon such programs as severance pay or supplementary unemployment benefits, which, it is true, affect only a part of
the workers, and which, it is also true, result in piecemeal development,
gaps, and overlap. But experiment is desirable in an area without private insurances.

In conclusion: The aggregate risk of unemployment is less than it
was a quarter of a century ago, though there are special risks today that
may be greater, particularly in the loss of skills. Today we have a first-
line-of-defense income maintenance program — unemployment insurance — that did not exist half a century ago. But looked at either in aggregate (extent of population covered) or in individual terms (percentage of income restored), economic unemployment is not a problem that
society has adjusted to as well as it has to premature death or old age.
We need to be flexible so as to maximize the gains that technological
change affords, including the benefits of automation. But we must cush-
ion the shock of insecurity, or we will never get anything but resistance
from those affected.

[31] See, for example, *Employment Security Review*, April, 1962, and July, 1962, which
provide analysis of federal area redevelopment and retraining legislation.

▪ OCCUPATIONAL
ILLNESS
AND ACCIDENTS

WITH this chapter we start to deal with the last of our insecurities, those brought about by sickness and accidental injury.

Accidental injury is the unplanned sudden event, sickness the same kind of phenomenon, but gradual. Sophisticated variations in defining these terms need not detain us; this common usage will be enough for our purposes. We shall use the term illness to cover both kinds of case.[1]

Sickness and accidental injury are the severest on the individual of any of the risks we have been talking about, death excepted (we are excluding here minor first-aid cases), for several reasons. If the blow falls upon the wage earner, income is interrupted, and, at the very same time, expenses increase because of the need for medical care. Permanent, even if only partial, disability may decrease future earning power. Finally, accidental injury and sickness are traumatic: they cause physical pain and perhaps psychological damage. This insecurity has all the unfortunate effects of the other kinds plus more of its own.

It is customary to divide accidental injury and sickness into two categories: the occupationally caused and the nonoccupationally caused. There is no logic behind such a distinction, since it may sometimes be difficult if not impossible to find the "cause." But there is a sound institutional basis for the distinction: a well-defined economic security program — workmen's compensation — exists and has existed for a half century to cover the occupationally caused illness, and we shall find it convenient to preserve the distinction and treat the two categories separately.

Two facts stand out regarding occupational illness. The preventive

[1] For a detailed discussion see "Origin and Program of the U.S. National Health Survey," *Health Statistics from the U.S. National Health Survey*, United States Department of Health, Education, and Welfare, United States Public Health Service (Series A-No. 1), 1958.

approach has been extremely successful dealing with it: deaths from industrial causes are, in absolute numbers, a third to half what they were fifty years ago in a labor force that has doubled during that time. Secondly, occupational illness called forth the first public social insurance program, workmen's compensation. Whereas public programs for old age and premature death and economic unemployment are little more than a quarter of a century old, workmen's compensation has over a half century of history. But this very social response is increasingly criticized. Says one leading work on the subject: "Once the pioneer trail blazer in social insurance, workmen's compensation has, like many other types of social legislation, not proved adaptable enough to keep abreast of a changing environment." [2] Another scholar says, "every recent evaluation of workmen's compensation has emphasized the gaps and weaknesses in the protective and restorative standards of the laws, and has viewed with increasing impatience the rate at which they move toward their objectives." [3]

Frequency

Two kinds of measurement, absolute figures and rates, are currently used to measure occupational injuries (which also embrace occupational sickness). These measures are of relatively recent origin, since the data about most manufacturing industries go back to the middle twenties, and those for the iron and steel industry go back to the turn of the century. But no one has attempted to carry summary accidental injury estimates back beyond these decades, as they have for the measurement of unemployment, and our comparisons must be more limited than they were for unemployment. Absolute measures include statistics on the following: *disabling work injury*, which, defined simply, is an injury (including death and permanent disabilities as listed below) that keeps the employee off the job for one full work shift or more; *permanent partial disability*, e.g., the loss of a finger; *permanent total disability*, which keeps a person from ever working again; *death*.

Table 29 presents data about these for selected years; such figures do not provide rates and therefore two additional measures have been devised: *frequency rate* (F.R.), the number of disabling work injuries per

[2] Herman M. and Anne R. Somers, *Workmen's Compensation*, New York: John Wiley, 1954, p. 269.
[3] Earl F. Cheit, *Injury and Recovery in the Course of Employment*, New York: John Wiley, 1961, p. 319.

Table 29. Occupational Injuries in 1910–15, 1939, and 1960

Disability	1910–15*	1939†	1960†
Disabling work injury	2,800,000	1,838,000	1,950,000
Permanent partial disability		109,400	82,200
Permanent total disability		1,800	1,300–1,500
Death	25,000–35,000	16,400	13,800

* 1913 estimates by Frederick L. Hoffman, "Industrial Accident Statistics," *Bulletin of the Bureau of Labor Statistics*, United States Department of Labor (Whole No. 157), March, 1915. (The disabling work injury figure was obtained by taking Hoffman's over-four-week disability group of 700,000 and adjusting to the one-shift concept.) For deaths, the 25,000 figure is from Hoffman; the 35,000 is cited on p. 153 of *Growth of Labor Law in the United States*, United States Department of Labor, 1962.

† 1939 and 1960 data from *Handbook of Labor Statistics*, United States Department of Labor, 1950, p. 179, and current releases.

Table 30. Accidental Injury Data, Selected Periods, 1910 to 1960

Year and Industry	Frequency	Year and Industry	Frequency
1910–14*		1938§ continued	
Iron and steel	59.2	Nonmanufacturing	
1930†		Engineering construction	
Bituminous coal	85.6	(high)	92.99
1960†		Telephonic communication	
Bituminous coal	42.4	(low)	2.64
1924‡		1958–60‖	
Manufacturing		Manufacturing	
Automobile tires (high) ..	98.64	Logging (high)	60.4
Boots and shoes (low) ...	4.96	Synthetic rubber (low) ..	1.4
1938§		Nonmanufacturing	
Manufacturing		Anthracite mining	
Logging (high)	107.47	(high)	60.8
Telephone (low)	2.36	Telephonic communication	
		(low)	0.7

* L. W. Chaney, "Statistics of Industrial Accidents in the U.S.," *Bulletin of the Bureau of Labor Statistics*, United States Department of Labor (Whole No. 425), January, 1925.

† 1930 and 1960 data from *Handbook of Labor Statistics*, United States Department of Labor, 1950, p. 179, and from current releases.

‡ "Accidents and Accident Rates in Selected Establishments in Specified Industries, 1924," *Bulletin 425*, January, 1925, Bureau of Labor Statistics, United States Department of Labor.

§ *Monthly Labor Review*, July, 1940.

‖ *Monthly Labor Review*, October, 1962; and *1959 Statistical Supplement to Monthly Labor Review*.

Table 31. Occupational Injuries and Deaths in Employed Labor
Force in 1910 and 1960

	1910 (Total Labor Force 34,200,000*)	1960 (Total Labor Force 66,700,000)
Disabling injury		
Total	2,800,000†	1,950,000
Per 1,000 of labor force ...	81	29
Death		
Total	25,000–35,000†	13,800
Per 1,000 of labor force ...	0.73–1.03	0.21

Source: Bureau of Labor Statistics, United States Department
of Labor, except as noted below.

* From Stanley Lebergott, "Annual Estimates of Unemployment in the United States, 1900–1954," *The Measurement and
Behavior of Unemployment*, Princeton: Princeton University
Press, 1957, pp. 215–16. (Unemployment rates were approximately the same in both years.)

† From F. L. Hoffman and other sources cited in Table 29.

million man hours of exposure, and *severity rate* (S.R.), the number of
days charged per million man hours of exposure, including charges for
permanent disability and death. The severity rate in effect measures the
seriousness of the injury. Since the same injury may have various impacts (as in healing time) a standard time charge is assigned; death,
for example, is assigned a 6,000-day loss. Comparing severity rates is
difficult because the rate base was changed in 1955 from one thousand
to one million hours of exposure, though we can, of course, make comparisons where the data exist by simply moving the decimal point three
places. High rates are found in mining, lumbering, and marine transportation, low rates in communications and business and educational
services. Certain industries such as mining, quarrying, and construction
are killers — the percentage of fatal to total cases is high; public utilities other than railroads rank low in fatal cases. The maiming industries
are railroading and agriculture, which have a high percentage of permanent disabilities to total cases. It is not possible to make the kinds of
1910–60 comparisons we would wish, but some current as well as past
contrasts are shown in Table 30.[4]

Absolutely and relatively, 1960 is compared with a half century ago

[4] For two graphic accounts of the problems of the past see Crystal Eastman, *Work-Ac-
cidents and the Law*, New York: Charities Publication Committee, 1910, and Alice Ham-
ilton, *Exploring the Dangerous Trades*, Boston: Little, Brown, 1943.

in Table 31. The improvement is clear, whether we look at disabling work injuries or death. One comparison may help to sharpen the differences: in 1913 there were 40 fatal accidents per 10,000 employed workers in manufacturing; in 1959 the rate had dropped to 1.2.[5]

Severity

Earlier in this chapter the term severity was used to refer to the seriousness of a work injury. We now wish to reapply the term, but this time in the same fashion as we did with other economic risks, namely with respect to income maintenance.

In premature death, old age, and economic unemployment, the income problems tend to be in one direction: income goes down, but expenses also tend to go down. The impact on income of occupational injury is more complex; three aspects of this complexity may be noted: (1) possible future diminution in earnings owing to permanent disability, as when a person loses a member or the use of a member; (2) the added expense required for treating the injury; (3) the income loss itself, caused by the inability of the injured person to continue working.

Let us look at these losses, first for 1960.[6] There appear to be no figures on the effect of permanent disability (1 above) upon future earning power. In the extreme cases — death or permanent total disability, which economically is its equivalent — the situation is like premature death. For permanent partial disability even conjecture is difficult, though a National Safety Council estimate suggests that a total of 120 million man days will be lost in future years because of 1961 work injuries (including permanent total cases).[7]

Estimated medical expenses (2 above) in the period around 1960 are as follows: The average medical cost per disabling work injury was $82 and $66 respectively in two midwestern states. These are not atypical, but they are perhaps on the high side for the nation as a whole.[8] For only those injuries in which the worker was absent for more than seven days, the costs were $400 and $257 respectively in the same two states.

[5] Computed from employment and accidental injury data used for Table 31.

[6] In premature death, old age, and economic unemployment it is not easy to obtain estimates of the *aggregate* loss (or "cost") to the economy. But for occupational injury, the National Safety Council, for example, makes annual cost estimates; for 1960 the Council estimated the total cost at about $4.4 billion.

[7] *Accident Facts*, National Safety Council, 1962, p. 24.

[8] These data have been kindly supplied by C. Arthur Williams, Jr.

Medical costs in 88 per cent of all cases were below $1,000; only 3.2 per cent reached $4,000 or above.[9]

The interruption of income — or income loss — occasioned by occupational injury should be of the same magnitude as that brought about by economic unemployment. Hence if we use the figures previously developed, the annual budget would be $4,200 and prorated on that basis for shorter periods.

We cannot compare 1910 and 1960 loss of earning power resulting from permanent disability. The added medical expense for 1910 we would estimate at $10 to $20.[10] The income loss would be as was estimated for unemployment — $540 to $765, depending upon the budget selected.

These are the income insecurities arising out of occupational injury. We turn now to the approaches society has taken to meet them.

The Preventive Ideal and the Reality

The preventive ideal is the same as that for premature death: elimination of occupational injury; conceptually elimination is not impossible, realistically it is. Some questions can be asked about the preventive approach. What will the future levels of occupational injury be? What role has workmen's compensation played in past reductions? What role is it likely to play in the future? Little information is available for predicting future levels of occupational injury, in contrast to labor force or population forecasts. But short-run variations are not difficult to predict in at least a directional sense. Disabling work injuries vary directly with the state of the economy and the class of new labor force entrants. Thus, in 1943, with a wartime economy and many

[9] This latter statistic is from Earl F. Cheit, *Medical Care under Workmen's Compensation*, United States Department of Labor, Bureau of Labor Standards (Bulletin 244), 1962, p. 13.

[10] Some evidence suggests this range may be too high. F. W. Loughran, M.D., medical adviser, New York State Insurance Fund, estimated that circa 1915 the American worker averaged nine days annual (workdays) loss through illness at a cost of $2.50 a day in average (daily) wage and $1.00 a day for medical attention. If we use a six-day workweek (three hundred days a year) then annual wages at $2.50 a day would be $750 a year, which approximates our estimates. But $9 total medical expense seems low to us, even allowing for much-reduced medical costs in 1910 compared with 1960, as well as for a lower intensity of use of medical services. See Dudley M. Holman, President, I.A.I.A.B.C., in his president's address, as contained in United States Department of Labor, Bureau of Labor Statistics, *Bulletin No. 248* (Workmen's Insurance and Compensation Series), March, 1919, pp. 11–15.

inexperienced workers, injuries reached an all-time high (2.4 million) for the years in which records were kept. In 1938, they were but 1.4 million, and in the fifties they ran between 1.8 and 2.1 million, with deaths and permanent disabilities staying approximately the same or drifting downward (deaths 13,100 in 1950, 13,800 in 1960; permanent disabilities 90,000 in 1940 and 82,200 in 1960). My guess is that disabling injury totals will not vary greatly in the near future, but that the other categories will continue to exhibit a slow downward drift.

The above figures are absolute. When they are converted to relative figures (i.e., when exposure is taken into account), the improvement is much more marked because what emerges is a steadily or gently declining incidence coupled with a growing labor force. For example, frequency rates in manufacturing were 15.3 in 1940, 20.0 in 1943, and 11.3 in 1960. This improvement, I believe, will continue.

To ask whether this improvement would have come about in the absence of workmen's compensation is to ask an iffy question not capable of a provable answer. The bulk of the evidence suggests the following:

1. Humanitarian considerations would have led to improvement; how much can only be guessed. The American safety movement antedated compensation, and employer, union, and government activity suggests that, compensation or not, preventive steps were being taken.

2. Workmen's compensation, with its financial reward of lower insurance rates (through experience rating) for the employer who improved his record, was instrumental as a preventive device. But care needs to be taken in making such a statement; safety improvement in railroading has kept pace with industry at large even though workmen's compensation was never applied to this industry. And prevention may be linked to employers' interest in such other factors as absenteeism and turnover.

3. Finally, as Herman and Anne Somers note, "it appears that compensation has a marked initial effect upon prevention activity, but that it eventually spends itself and other motivations must replace it." [11] What these may be in the future only time will tell.

Should we be doing better? Ideally, yes; we should have fewer disabling work injuries, deaths, and permanent disabilities. Realistically, the answer is also yes; better public and private programing would im-

[11] Somers and Somers, *op. cit.*, p. 233.

prove the record. Yet the historical pattern *is* one of programs of improvement.

The Alleviative Ideal and the Reality

The alleviative ideal would be to maintain income at the nondeferrable expense level during the period of disability, to cover medical costs incurred because of the injury, and to indemnify the permanently partly disabled worker for any future reduction in earning power. How well do our current programs meet this ideal? How well do they meet the far more realistic ideal of maintaining the income at the two-thirds level?

The first point to note is that current programs use "multiple methods of dealing with work injury [and] form a crazy-quilt design." [12] The three principal methods include state workmen's compensation acts, currently operating in all jurisdictions; federal legislation, including a complicated pattern of statutes such as the Federal Employees' Compensation Act, the Longshoremen's and Harbor Workers' Compensation Act, and special acts for merchant seamen (covering both compensation and the right to sue) and interstate railroad workers (giving the right to sue); state employers' liability and tort law in which intrastate cases not covered by workmen's compensation *may* be processed.[13] The word may is used advisedly here, because in such cases the employee may be required to bring suit, and at the state level the effectiveness of this procedure is debatable; the number of settlements appears extremely small.

Two kinds of estimate of the degree of coverage provided by these three forms of protection can be given. The first kind uses the "potentially eligible" approach. Here the civilian labor force is used as a base and from it are subtracted the unemployed, the self-employed, and unpaid family workers — groups who by the nature of their employment logically would not be eligible for compensation. This potentially eligible group is a fairly constant part of the civilian labor force, recently averaging some 78 to 80 per cent. For 1960 the number of workers covered in an average month by workmen's compensation (broadly defined) ranged from 43.9 to 44.1 million, or 78.8 per cent of the 55.8 million ci-

[12] Cheit, *op. cit.*, p. 25.
[13] I view this third category as unsatisfactory because it was the method for which workmen's compensation was introduced as a more desirable alternative. But since it is a form now in use, I include it in my discussion.

Table 32. Workmen's Compensation Coverage in
1910 and 1960 (in millions)

	1910	1960
Total labor force	36.5*	73.1†
Total civilian labor force	36.4‡	70.6†
Less self-employed	10.2§	9.3†
Less unemployed	2.2*	3.9†
Less unpaid family workers	1.5§	1.4†
Difference	13.9	14.6
Potentially eligible for workmen's compensation	22.5‖	56.0‖
Total employees covered by workmen's compensation	.1**	43.9–44.1††
Percentage of employed civilian labor force covered	<1.0%	66%
Percentage of potentially eligible covered	<1.0%	79%

* Stanley Lebergott as cited in Table 31.

† *Employment and Earnings*, United States Department of Labor, Bureau of Labor Statistics.

‡ Armed forces personnel (100,000) in 1910 as indicated in *Historical Statistics of the United States* (1960), p. 736.

§ Arthur Reede, *Adequacy of Workmen's Compensation*, Cambridge: Harvard University Press, 1947, p. 17.

‖ Computed by subtracting exclusions from civilian force.

** Based upon data in Reede (above) and *Bulletin of the Bureau of Labor Statistics*, United States Department of Labor (Whole No. 77), 1908, p. 334.

†† A. M. Skolnik, "New Benchmarks in Workmen's Compensation," *Social Security Bulletin*, June, 1962, p. 5.

vilian wage and salary earners. The balance were covered by employers' liability and tort law.[14]

If one uses the total employed civilian labor force as a base, the degree of coverage is less. This is to be expected: the self-employed, for example, would not be eligible for workmen's compensation in its usual sense; yet these workers can be and are injured at work, and their insecurity is thus no different. In 1960 the employed civilian labor force was 66.4 million, and 43.9 to 44.1 million (the covered group) was 66 per cent of it.

The picture is summarized — and data for 1910 introduced as well — in Tables 32 and 33. The year 1910 is a satisfactory comparison date in one respect, unsatisfactory in another. It is, of course, one of the ter-

[14] See Alfred M. Skolnik, "New Benchmarks in Workmen's Compensation," *Social Security Bulletin*, June, 1962, p. 5.

Table 33. How Occupational Illness Was Met in 1910 and 1960

Category	1910	1960
Potentially eligible for workmen's compensation (millions)	22.5	56.0
Covered by workmen's compensation (millions)	.1	44.0
Potentially eligible covered by workmen's compensation	<1.0%	79%
Covered by employer's liability and tort law (millions)	22.4	12.0
Potentially eligible covered by employer's liability and tort law	99.6%	21.0%
Total civilian labor force not potentially eligible for workmen's compensation (millions)	13.9	14.6
Civilian labor force not eligible for workmen's compensation	38.2%	20.7%
Total civilian labor force not eligible for or not covered by workmen's compensation (millions)	36.3	26.6
Civilian labor force not eligible for or not covered by workmen's compensation	99.7%	37.7%

Source: Computed from data in Table 32. There are some legal niceties about dual coverage under workmen's compensation and tort laws. The rule appears to be — notwithstanding the exclusive-remedy nature of workmen's compensation — that the employee is also eligible for liability and tort claims if the employer is negligent. Thus in *Jones vs. Sheffield Steel Co.*, cited in 29 *NAACA Law Journal* 425 (1962), a jury awarded a $250,000 settlement to an injured employee (in addition to $12,000 under the Texas workmen's compensation law) because the employer was negligent.

minal years used in this study and therefore it permits parallel treatment. But it is also just before the emergence of a real workmen's compensation law: in 1910 there was a federal law and two state laws (both of which were subsequently held unconstitutional); in 1911, nine states enacted laws, in 1912 three, in 1913 eight; and by 1920 all but eight states. We are thus dealing with a problem right at a dividing line in its history.

Before inquiring into the income maintenance and medical expense features of workmen's compensation, it may be useful to describe certain of its basic characteristics as they applied to those 44.0 million covered employees in 1960.

First, the disability in question must be compensable; nearly all injuries are, but not all diseases. An employee may thus be covered by workmen's compensation, but his occupational disability may be a disease the state law in question does not apply to.

Second, if compensable in the sense that the law is applicable, the disability must "arise out of and be in the course of employment." The interpretation of this apparently simple statement has become most tortured, but its meaning is clear: it means occupational injury.

Third, the "remedy," workmen's compensation, is (with exceptions) exclusive, meaning that if the injured employee accepts the compensation approach he is (with exceptions) not entitled to make use also of other methods (such as a suit for damages against the employer) to collect additional recompense.[15] The exclusiveness of the remedy does not, however, exclude or preclude the payment of supplements. If all medical costs are compensable one would not find supplementation, for in such a case supplements would amount to duplicate payments. But wage (or income) supplementation exists and continues to increase. The current practice is to have the income restored under workmen's compensation deducted from whatever total is payable from other sources.[16] This is in contrast to unemployment compensation practices and results primarily from the fact that these injury plans have not been collectively bargained.

Recovery of Medical Expenses, Today and Yesterday

In trying to generalize about unemployment compensation we noted the difficulties resulting from pulling data together from over half a hundred state laws. The problem is compounded in the case at hand, for we not only have a more complex security program (state and federal statutes and tort law) but in place of a single insecurity (unemployment) there are various forms of the one insecurity: death, perma-

[15] The major exceptions are cases where the employer is negligent (see the source material in Table 33). Since 1958, however, an additional possibility of duplicating income maintenance payments has appeared. Under the disability income payments of OASDI it is possible in the absence of state law to the contrary to collect for permanent total disability under both OASDI and workmen's compensation. Before 1958 an offset provision appeared in the federal law. The problem is not quantitatively important at the moment, but it could well develop into a serious issue.

[16] This is, in effect, a SUB plan for occupational injury. Problem cases, as they arise, are not so much a consequence of supplementation as of substitution. A sizable number of employees (over 25 million in 1960) are covered by plans providing temporary disability assistance for nonoccupational injury. These plans are often more liberal than workmen's compensation and it is not unknown for a worker injured on the job to claim he was injured off the job.

nent total disability, permanent partial disability, temporary total disability. Let us see, however, if we cannot go a little way toward pulling the bits and pieces together.

Table 34 provides information about the sources of income restoration in 1910 and 1960 during occupational illness. The 1960 figure for workmen's compensation recovery appears slightly low: the program covers some 66 per cent of the employed civilian labor force, yet compensates for 50–60 per cent of the work injuries. The reason could be that occupational illness is less concentrated in those areas covered by workmen's compensation. The table does suggest, however, that in 1910 "formal" income restoration was available for fewer than a quarter of the cases, whereas in 1960 it was available to many more.

But what part of wages lost and added medical expense were covered? In addition to the difference between the two periods (1910 versus 1960), the kind of illness (death versus temporary total disability) and the applicable economic security program (workmen's compensation versus damage suit) make a difference. Let us look first at medical expenses and then at wage restoration.[17]

Earlier in this chapter it was suggested that the average medical expense for occupational illness was on the order of $10–$20 in 1910, $60–$80 in 1960.

In 1910 15 to 25 per cent of occupational illness cases were compensated through tort law or such other formal means as self-insurance or health insurance. An analysis of payments made in death, permanent disability, and temporary cases suggests the following: In deaths that were compensated, both medical and burial expenses were met.[18] Permanent disability involves no burial expense, but medical costs could be greater — let us arbitrarily assume they totaled $300. With a mean payment of $2,000 to the permanently disabled who were compensated (less attorney's fees of $500) medical costs would be met (again only

---

[17] Economic and social logic is not always consistent. With respect to some insecurities, such as unemployment, it contends that the individual ought to be responsible (in effect through "personal co-insurance") for meeting part of his upkeep while jobless. In occupational illness, however, it is regarded as perfectly proper for a program such as workmen's compensation to pay all medical expenses. Though there are some sound reasons for this (as in the incentive effect), there are also some inconsistencies.

[18] Total expenses averaged $200 for burial and $110–$120 for medical care where relevant. The mean total tort liability payment was $1,000, of which $250 was for attorney's fees. The balance more than covered total expenses. Data are from J. Harrington Boyd as cited in Table 34.

Table 34. Occupational Injuries Receiving Some Wage
Compensation after a 1-Week Waiting Period in 1910
and 1960 by Source of Compensation*

	1910	1960
Total cases (millions) †	2.8†	1.950†
Compensated by workmen's compensation	0%‡	50–60%§
Compensated by tort and liability law	10–13%‖	2–5%**
Covered by other means; explicit income restoration††	5–12%	5–20%
Total percentages	15–25%	57–85%

* Some work injuries may be compensated by more than one of the above means. Conversely, some 40 per cent of the work injuries would have no wage restoration (though medical expenses would be covered) since there is commonly a one-week waiting period (as is also true in unemployment insurance) and these 40 per cent lost "less than a week of work."

† From data cited in Table 29. Some evidence suggests that the "disabling work injury" statistics underreport the problem. For example, the National Health Survey in recent years has reported approximately 4,200,000 (annual) activity-restricting injuries occurring at work. Even after allowing for differences in definition, the variance is considerable.

‡ Based on the fact that only 75,000 workers were eligible for workmen's compensation in 1910.

§ We took data from *Accident Facts*, 1962 edition, reporting the number of work injuries compensated in 1960 by some reporting districts. We then assumed the compensation in reporting and nonreporting districts was proportional to employment. Thirty-two reporting districts having an employment of 45,011,443 out of a total employment of 64,-639,247 reported 971,174 cases compensated in 1960. Some reporting districts were not used in the calculation. Using this methodology we arrived at the conclusion that 70–75 per cent of all disabling work injuries were compensated by workmen's compensation. Because of differences in the reporting of injuries by the Bureau of Labor Statistics and the National Health Survey we adjusted our estimates downward.

‖ Based on the testimony of J. Harrington Boyd, Chairman of the Employer's Liability Commission of Ohio, United States Congress, United States Senate, Employer's Liability and Workmen's Compensation Commission, *Hearings before the Employer's Liability and Workmen's Compensation Commission* (62nd Congress, 2nd Session, Senate Document No. 13, Volume 2), 1912.

** Since so many accidents are compensated by workmen's compensation, and since accidents to the self-employed are not subject to liability-tort action (that is, they cannot sue themselves), this estimate is not too low.

†† These other means include self-insurance, health insurance, company supplements, and government welfare programs.

for those compensated) .[19] In temporary total disability a similar result obtains: for medical expenses of $10–$20, payment averaged $75, with attorney's charges of $20, allowing a net of $55, sufficient to cover charges (for that minority compensated) .

Our knowledge of payment from other sources such as health insurance is less complete, but that kind of payment was probably no greater.

Medical expense as covered by workmen's compensation laws in 1960 can be summarized as shown in Table 35. The 1960 picture was, however, much less bleak than this table might suggest. Only about 59 per cent of covered employees have unlimited medical coverage. Moreover, the $60–$80 average expense for 1960 is well within the limits set by *all* jurisdictions which limit such care. Bleak or not in the aggregate, for a small minority who incur more medical expenses than the limits allow — perhaps fewer than 4 or 5 per cent — the picture is grim. These are the people really afflicted.

Table 35. Medical Benefits for Accidental Injury Available to Employees Covered by Workmen's Compensation, 1960

Limitations on Medical Benefits	Workers Covered	
	No.	%
No arbitrary limits	24,651,500	58.9
Arbitrary limits		
Agency can extend indefinitely in all cases	6,502,000	15.5
Agency can extend indefinitely in certain cases	5,380,000	12.9
Agency can grant extensions only	3,385,500	8.1
No extensions possible	1,935,000	4.6

Source: Earl F. Cheit, *Medical Care under Workmen's Compensation*, United States Department of Labor, Bureau of Labor Standards (Bulletin 244) , 1962, p. 10.

To summarize: In 1910, with no public program, approximately a fifth of the occupationally injured were either protected by some private means such as insurance or recovered some money through tort actions. In cases of death and permanent and temporary disability, awards, *when made*, tended to cover medical expenses. We can therefore conclude that in 1910 a fifth of the occupationally injured received money enough to cover their expenses. Or, differently stated, 80 out of

[19] See United States Congress, House of Representatives, *Federal Accident Compensation Act* (62nd Congress, 2nd Session, Volume 1, House Report N.1441) , 1913, p. 22.

100 of them received nothing toward their medical expenses; the remaining 20 were paid enough to meet their medical expenses.

In 1960 the picture is perceptibly better, notwithstanding the criticisms leveled at workmen's compensation and other programs. Except for certain self-employed or equivalent categories, public programs such as workmen's compensation cover 80 per cent of the potentially eligible labor force. We might further assume that much of the "ineligible" labor force is covered by such means as private insurance. We might suggest, therefore, that about 80 per cent of the civilian labor force is protected more or less completely as respects medical expense caused by occupational illness. Of the remainder, some are not likely to be protected by their employer (agricultural workers or domestic servants), whereas others in the self-employed category may be similarly unprotected by formal programs. If we use here the "net equity" approach developed earlier (Table 8) we have a sum of $300 per married couple in 1910 and $4,300 in 1960. In both years the average person not protected by formal plans would have something by way of personal resources to assist in illness. One weakness in this reasoning is that the "average unprotected individual" is likely to be the migrant laborer or the domestic servant whose net equity is likely to be very low if not nonexistent. Also unfortunate is the person with "average" resources but far above-average medical expense.

An index in dollars of medical expense coverage for occupational illness for these two times would be as follows: *ideal*: 100 per cent of medical costs; *1910*: 5–15 per cent, *1960*: 75–80 per cent. This includes private as well as public protection; they were probably close together in 1960 in the level of expense coverage they afforded.

Recovery of Wages, Today and Yesterday

Let us turn now to the picture of wage and salary maintenance consequent upon occupational illness in 1910 and in 1960. Again it will be desirable to distinguish among the range of disabilities, death to temporary.

Table 34 indicated that 15–25 per cent of all occupational illness cases received some compensation in 1910. We have previously noted the level of protection provided in the area of medical expenses; here our concern is with wage and salary maintenance.

In death cases compensated, the mean payment was $1,000, of which

108

$200 must be subtracted for funeral expenses and $250 for attorney's fees, leaving $550.[20] An annual nondeferrable budget for this period ranged from $540 to $765; the family thus had about a year's wages restored. If we assume that the deceased was midway through a fifty-year work span (ages 15 to 65), his death at 40 deprived him of 25 working years. Income restoration was thus on the order of 4 per cent.

In cases of permanent disability in 1910 recovery averaged $2,000, of which attorney's fees were $500; deducting $300 for typical medical expenses, we have $1,200 — a little more or less than two years' wage restoration.[21] If we assume the disability to be total and the worker's age to be 40 (as in the death case), then income restoration was about 10 per cent. Permanent partial disabilities are harder to analyze. If a worker lost a little finger, received a $2,000 payment, and was not diminished in future earning power, he would stand to gain. One may believe, though, that in cases of this kind recovery would have been much less than $2,000 — if, indeed, any damages were obtainable.

In temporary disability cases in 1910, recovery averaged $75; subtracting attorney's fees of $20 we have $55, which would cover medical expenses and leave $35–$40, an amount that would cover three or four weeks of lost income. If the majority of cases were four-week-or-less disabilities, this payment covered the wage loss. (It should be recalled, however, that payment was made in only about a fifth of all cases.)

Data for 1960 are much more readily available than for 1910, although again a diversity of programs makes simple comparisons difficult.

In death cases for 1960 Cheit found that the median benefit for fifty-one jurisdictions replaced 18 per cent of the loss; sixteen jurisdictions replaced 20 or more per cent, nine 15 or less. If other benefits (OASDI, private insurance, and so on) are included, the replacement was 34.4 per cent for California cases for 1956.[22] Berkowitz found that in 1957 average total death benefits varied from $8,600 in Mississippi to $63,-700 in Hawaii.[23] If we take the $4,200 budget for 1960 (p. 99) and ad-

[20] These and other 1910 data are derived from J. Harrington Boyd as cited in Table 34.

[21] It is interesting to note that permanent disability afforded a basis for greater recovery than death. The evidence suggests two reasons: death was a clean break, whereas permanent disability often left a living shell, in physical and mental pain, and permanent disability frequently necessitated continued medical care.

[22] Cheit, *op. cit.*, pp. 108–09; 112–15.

[23] Monroe Berkowitz, *Workmen's Compensation: The New Jersey Experience*, New Brunswick: Rutgers University Press, 1960, p. 56.

just for the earlier year (1957), we arrive at $4,000–$4,100. Using the Berkowitz data, this suggests that the number of years of wages restored ranged from two to fifteen, or a percentage restoration (assuming the worker was forty when killed) of 4 to 60. Thus during the half century there has been some rise in the level of recovery in death benefit cases, though the situation in 1960 was far from ideal. The major improvement has been not so much in the level of payment for those who were paid, but rather in the numbers of those who were paid some damages. In 1910 it appears that in only 20 per cent of the death cases was payment made; by 1960 the percentage is 80 per cent or higher.

In permanent disability cases in 1960 the evidence suggests recovery of less than two fifths of the total wage loss.[24] For 1958 Cheit says that twenty-four states offset less than 20 per cent of the loss; seven jurisdictions offset more than 40 per cent. Again the improvement since 1910 is primarily in the number of those receiving benefits rather than in the level of benefits received.

For temporary disability cases in 1960 the following information is applicable. In the thirty-seven programs without dependents' allowances, the average percentage of wages replaced was 50.1 per cent. In fifteen programs with dependents' allowances, recovery was 49.2 per cent. For a worker with the maximum number of dependents, the rate of compensation was 64.7 per cent. Because workmen's compensation benefits are not subject to federal income or social security taxes, the percentages of take-home pay replaced by the average benefit was higher. A worker with no dependents earning the average 1960 weekly wage of $93.34, and with standard deductions, would have had 62 per cent of his take-home pay restored. A married man with two children (and thus with higher take-home pay) would have had 56 per cent restored in states without dependents' allowances and 67 per cent in states with them.[25]

If we take into account the waiting period (usually seven days) that all jurisdictions (except Oregon) have, the rate of recovery is less, except when a case lasts beyond a certain time (such as twenty-two days) when retroactivity is applied. Using a three-week period of disability (which is close to the average nineteen-calendar-day duration of temporary cases) Skolnik computed that the amount of wages restored

[24] A. M. Skolnik, *op. cit.*, pp. 10–12.
[25] *Ibid.*, pp. 10–11.

110

during the three weeks was 37.3 per cent for a single worker. He concludes that workmen's compensation was leaving unmet, in 1960, more than three fifths of the total wage loss in temporary disability cases.[26] Using a nondeferrable-budget approach, the degree of recovery appears higher, as pointed out in Table 36 on the following page.

We saw in our discussion of unemployment that some employees were covered by Supplemental Unemployment Benefits and that these benefits could be paid in addition to unemployment insurance. A study by Harland Fox provides similar information in the occupational illness category.[27] Fox notes that in 1959 some 39.3 million employees were covered by group life insurance; 19.7 million by accidental death and dismemberment insurance; and 20.9 million by wage replacement sickness insurance. But this "corporate social security system" (including group hospital and medical insurance) is almost exclusively concerned with providing *nonoccupational* sickness benefits. Death benefits are customarily added to those received under workmen's compensation, and the same is true for permanent disability cases; but the offset plan is the most common in temporary disability: the workmen's compensation payment is offset against the private payment, and only if the private payment is higher does the person receive a supplement. Fox believes that corporate benefits are at about the same level as those from workmen's compensation and supplements of minor importance.

The Ideal and the Reality of Wage Restoration

The income maintenance problem in occupational illness is more complex than in other areas for two reasons. First, because universal coverage of occupational illness is less easily accomplished by a public program like workmen's compensation than is universal coverage of another insecurity — old age, for example — by a public program like OASDI, because of the existence of such groups as the self-employed, the possibility of a uniform floor of public protection is less. Second, the problem is more complex because private coverings on the floor of pro-

---

[26] It should be noted, however, that temporary disability or not, workmen's compensation payments last longer than unemployment compensation. The latter's duration is about 26–39 weeks. For temporary disability cases, workmen's compensation is frequently payable for as long as five years.

[27] "Corporate Supplements to Workmen's Compensation," in E. F. Cheit and Margaret S. Gordon, eds., *Occupational Disability and Public Policy*, New York: John Wiley, 1963, pp. 334–365.

tection in occupational illness are not so customary as they are for other insecurities. If you retire, for example, it is not uncommon for you to have some private supplementation to your OASDI protection. But if you suffer an occupational injury it is much less likely that you will have a private policy to augment your workmen's compensation payment. There is one major exception: occupational death calls forth the additional protection afforded by whatever life insurance the deceased had (including group policies at the place of employment), as well as "retirement" income.

It may be suggested, in the absence of a logical extension of universal

Table 36. An Income Restoration Index Expressed as Percentages of Nondeferrable Budget in Occupational Illness in 1910 and 1960

	Ideal	1910	1960
*Fatalities**			
Public programs: workmen's compensation†	67%, then 50%	1-2%	18%
Private means and such private programs as exist	33%, then 50%	5-10%‡	35%‡
Total	100%	6-12%	53%
Permanent Total Disabilities			
Public programs: workmen's compensation†	100%§	2-4%	30%
Private means and such private programs as exist		1-2%†	5-12%
Total	100%	3-6%	35-42%
Temporary Disabilities			
Public programs: workmen's compensation†	67%‖	1-2%	55%
Private means and such private programs as exist	33%	13%†	17%‡
Total	100%	14-15%	72%

* Fatalities should be treated as premature deaths were in the second chapter.

† Were a separate index to be developed for those not covered by public programs (that is, covered only by their own insurance), I believe the degree of income restoration would be less, since I believe that proportionately fewer of such people carry income loss protection and that tort law protection is incomplete.

‡ These estimates have been developed from data in Tables 11 and 28. The permanent total case is frequently the most serious since life insurance proceeds are not available in the same way as for premature death. Moreover, there is another person to be taken care of (unlike the departed in the case of premature death).

§ The seriousness of the permanent total case justifies, we believe, 100 per cent indemnity. Rehabilitation should be utilized as fully as possible.

‖ The permanent partial case (which is, in its total impact, only temporary) might be given special indemnification for the loss of, or loss of use of, bodily members. For regular temporary cases we would apply the customary one-week waiting period, to be indemnified if the illness lasts beyond three or four weeks.

coverage under workmen's compensation, private enterprise has an obligation to provide forms of insurance that would cover the excluded groups with the same kind of protection that protects those covered by workmen's compensation. This obligation has in fact already been met and the self-employed, for example, can secure such protection by charging the premium as a cost of production. Whether they and others like them have in fact bought protection is another question.

For those covered by public programs, income maintenance should be at the level of two thirds of the nondeferrable budget, in contrast to the half recommended for other insecurities. The reason is the absence of readily available private supplements (except in the event of death) to be laid upon the public floor of protection.

A wage restoration index for 1910 and 1960, using primarily data for workmen's compensation and allied public programs, is shown in Table 36. This is a more limited kind of tabulation than we developed for earlier chapters, principally because there are few or no private supplements for this insecurity, as there are for the programs earlier analyzed. (And, as we have seen, where supplements are found, an offset principle is used.)

An Evaluation: The Risks, The Programs

Let us now pull together the threads of thought about occupational illness: This insecurity decreased both absolutely and relatively in the half century from 1910 to 1960. Deaths alone decreased by half, or, if we take into account the doubling of the labor force, by three quarters. In 1910 but three infant public programs existed; by 1960, workmen's compensation provided a floor of protection. In 1910 recovery of medical expense was 5–15 per cent for all those injured; by 1960 it was 75–80 per cent. In 1910 wage restoration for all classes of cases approximated 2 per cent; by 1960 it was twelve times that. In the face of this degree of improvement I am nevertheless critical, essentially because I believe the improvement could be much greater. My criticism of workmen's compensation as a public program can be summed up as follows:

This kind of social legislation, like many others, has not proved adaptable to changing circumstances. The coverage has failed to be extended to some 20 per cent of those potentially eligible, has not been extended to occupational disease to the same degree as to occupational injury, and has failed to keep pace with increasing wages, leading to an

113

erosion of income maintenance and, in effect, a "flat benefit" schedule. Comprehensive coverage has not been extended to workers suffering large wage losses or high medical expense. Nor has the rehabilitative approach accomplished what many critics believe it could do. There has been a tendency for the program to became a battleground of litigation rather than a means for efficient processing of claims, and desired improvements have become a matter of legislative logrolling rather than of rational decision-making.

We might conclude as we did in the chapter on unemployment compensation that the workmen's compensation program is here to stay, that "federalization," as a means of simplifying change and improvement, is not at all likely, and that all we can do is patiently and persistently to work for improvement.

Alternative approaches, such as the damage suit approach used in the railroad industry, are less susceptible of the kind of specific criticism applied above. On the one hand, they use the very approach that workmen's compensation sought to replace; on the other, railroad employees and their representatives have resisted all efforts to make the replacement. These alternative approaches thus cannot be really unsatisfactory.

The private program supplements to (or substitutes for, in the case of the potentially ineligible) public programs are more difficult to evaluate and criticize. One may suggest that satisfactory approaches (such as insurance) exist; satisfactory forms of insurance policies have been devised and used; the record of the insurance industry appears satisfactory in such matters as costs and claims processing; and the main problem is the ignorance and lethargy found wherever voluntary individual action must be taken.

In conclusion, then: Has there been improvement? Yes, very much. Has it been all that could have been done? By no means. The future? With the diversities and conflicts of a state-by-state approach, I do not expect to see occupational illness as the economic insecurity in which major improvements will be made in the near future.

■ NONOCCUPATIONAL
ILLNESS

Two preliminary comments must be made about nonoccupational illness. Data are more difficult to come by in this area than in any of the others thus far examined. And the available figures are sometimes cast in a form different from those used previously. The net effect of these two facts is to make analysis more complex and comparison less satisfactory. In premature death, old age, economic unemployment, and occupational illness, public programs provide the floor of protection, private programs the supplements. In nonoccupational illness, there is no basic public income and medical expense program, though there has been since 1957 a public floor of protection for long-term income loss, namely the disability insurance feature of OASDI; there is some public short-term income protection through temporary disability laws; and there are some special medical assistance plans. The roles of public and private programs are here just reversed, or at the very least, private plans seek to do in this area of insecurity what public plans do in others. This difference causes variations we shall encounter in the subsequent discussion.

The Data Problem

Quantifying nonoccupational illness is much more difficult than quantifying premature death for three reasons, two of which we already noted in connection with economic unemployment; the third is new. It will be worthwhile, however, to re-examine the general line of argument.[1]

Conceptually and dimensionally premature death and old age are easy to distinguish, unemployment less so, and illness very difficult. Is a minor cut an accidental injury; is a cold a sickness? Some external criteria might be applied — an illness is an illness only if it results in lost work or treatment that costs money — but at present we do not have such criteria. Second, though it may not be difficult to identify an

[1] See the discussion in Turnbull, Williams, and Cheit, *op. cit.*, pp. 297–302.

accidental injury, some may feign sickness and others really sick will claim they are not.

Like unemployment, illness has a time dimension; a person may be ill more than once during any period. But unlike unemployment itself, illness may run the entire spectrum from minor to critically serious. Any probability structure would therefore be complex even if the specific probabilities were ascertainable.

Births, deaths, unemployment, and certain illnesses such as the contagious ones are measured and reported regularly, but most illnesses are not. Such data as we have come from periodic surveys or prevalence studies, and up to now such surveys have not been made systematically as the decennial population census has. Nor have these surveys been made by a single agency such as the Bureau of the Census; they are rather the result of the activities of various public and private agencies. Finally, these surveys have not been cast in the same mold; comparisons are more difficult than for unemployment.[2]

Two kinds of information are relevant to a discussion of illness and its impacts: the nature of illness and changes over the years in its causal forces, and the amount of illness — its frequency and severity.

The Nature of Illness

We earlier divided illness into accidental injury and sickness. Let us now look at the changing character of these causes of economic insecurity.

Accidental injury is influenced by man's environment and the tools he uses. In 1910 there were only 800 deaths in the entire United States from automobile accidents; in 1960, the figure was over 38,000. Conversely, whatever the figure in 1910, deaths owing to runaway horses must have dropped to close to zero by 1960. Fatalities from commercial airline accidents in 1910 were zero; in 1960 there were 328.

One might suggest that life is a kind of race. The more complex it becomes in the goods and services man uses — power boats or power mowers — the greater the possibility of accidental injury. The race is slowed by efforts at control — safety education or restrictions (as in setting a minimum age for driving).

[2] In 1956 Congress authorized the Public Health Service to begin a continuous survey of health conditions in the United States. From 1958 on we therefore have some comparable data, particularly in the acute conditions and disability categories.

116

Table 37. Death Rate Per 100,000 by Decade from 1910 to 1960

Year	All Causes	Cardio-vascular Diseases	Malig-nant Neo-plasms	Certain Diseases of Early Infancy	Influenza, Pneu-monia	Accidents	All Other
1910	1,468.0	287.2	76.2	73.0	155.0	84.2	791.5
1920	1,298.9	282.5	83.4	69.2	207.3	70.0	586.5
1930	1,132.1	327.8	97.4	49.6	102.5	79.8	475.0
1940	1,076.4	406.6	120.3	39.2	70.3	73.2	366.9
1950	963.8	494.4	139.8	40.5	31.3	60.6	197.3
1960	945.7	512.0	147.4	37.0	36.6	51.9	160.8

Source: *Annual Vital Statistics of the United States and Monthly Vital Statistics Report,* United States Department of Health, Education, and Welfare; Public Health Service, National Vital Statistics Division. Figures may not add up exactly because of rounding.

Sickness is a much more complex problem, resulting from and responding to more numerous and more remote factors.[3] The difficulties of providing data about it, quantitative or qualitative, are immense, for two reasons: the problem of diagnosis — defining the kind of sickness and the problem of reporting — getting the information, whatever the classification system used. Despite the somewhat unsatisfactory evidence, it is possible to derive certain generalizations about the trends: Communicable diseases have declined steadily. The annual rate per 100,000 population for diphtheria was 139.0 in 1912, and less than 1.0 in 1960. In fact, in 1960 with a population of 180.6 million people, fewer than 1,000 cases were reported in the United States. Smallpox fell from 30.8 in 1912 to 0 in 1960, typhoid fever from 81.8 to less than 1.0. There has been a sizable decrease in the incidence of certain infectious diseases in younger people and a sizable rise in the proportion of deaths among older persons. In effect, we have changed from a society of childhood diseases to one of old age affliction.[4] This is also evident from the statistics (Table 37).[5]

[3] A most useful volume here is Alfred E. Cohn and Claire Lingg, *The Burden of Diseases in the United States,* New York: Oxford University Press, 1950.

[4] This kind of development poses interesting measurement problems. When we noted in the second chapter that mortality rates had decreased we did not imply that people now live forever, or, even from age 60 on, that their life expectancy was much greater. Fewer die in the earlier years today compared with yesterday, but this means more must die later.

[5] The interested reader may consult Cohn and Lingg, *op. cit.,* and also Mortimer Spiegelman, *Significant Mortality and Morbidity Trends since 1900,* Philadelphia: American College of Life Underwriters, 1951.

Frequency and Severity

A variety of specialized frequency and severity data may be found, but comparisons tend to be difficult, because until recently the series embodying these data have been short-lived. One can get, however, for recent years such frequency measures as annual days of disability per 1,000 population by age and the illness producing the disability, or such severity measures as surgical cases or length of hospital stay or days of disability per given exposure unit.[6]

A more useful set of incidence data for long-run comparison purposes is found in Figure 2, from which we build up the following presentation.

A half century ago military personnel were sick about 10 days a year. If we include accidental injury as contributing a third again as much, the total would be about 14 days a year.[7] By 1960 this total dropped to about 5 days a year — a decline of almost two thirds. It has been suggested that trends of sickness and nonbattle injury in the armed services are similar to trends of diseases and accidents in the civilian population of comparable ages.[8] In absolute terms Figure 2 shows the death rates for the civilian and military groups running close together. Current data suggest, however, that illness rates are higher for civilians, perhaps because, for one thing, the selection process draws healthier people into the military or because of the supervised diet in the armed forces. The best estimate I can make is that civilian rates are currently about 40 per cent higher than military and were 50 per cent higher around 1910. This would mean 15 days a year in 1910, fewer than 7 in 1960.

If we equate days in bed with days sick, then current estimates from different sources come very close to each other. We estimated fewer than 7 days above; bed-days for 1960 average out to 6-plus per person (5.3 for males, 6.7 for females).[9] If, however, we broaden the notion of sick to include restricted activity days, the figures for 1960 are 14 for males, 18 for females. If we carry these figures back to 1910 I do not be-

[6] Public health data indicate that respiratory ailments lead in the frequency pattern; diseases of the heart and mental and neurological causes produce the greatest number of days of disability; and tonsillectomies and accidents produce the most surgical cases.

[7] For accident data upon which we base our estimates see the table on accidents in current *Health, Education, and Welfare Indicators.*

[8] This method of analysis (and comparison) may well be open to question; our only defense is that it is the best we can work up.

[9] See *Health, Education, and Welfare Trends,* 1962 ed., p. 20.

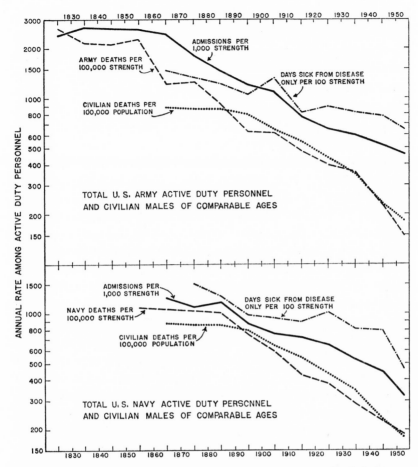

Figure 2. Long-time average trends in army and navy annual admissions to sick report, annual days sick, and annual deaths (exclusive of battle casualties and exceptionally high peaks of illness and death due to epidemics, nonbattle loss of ships, and other disasters), 1830–1953, with trend added to 1960. The source of these data is Selwyn D. Collins, "Illness of Employed Civilians and Military Personnel," *A Review and Study of Illness and Medical Care with Special Reference to Long-Time Trends*, United States Department of Health, Education, and Welfare, United States Public Health Service, Public Health Monograph 48, 1957; extrapolations to 1960 from *Health, Education, and Welfare Indicators.*

119

lieve they would more than double, as days sick, reported above, did. This lack of parity results from the nature of the causes of restricted activity; these have not changed markedly over the half century. An estimate of restricted activity days for 1910 would suggest perhaps 25 days for females, 22 for males.

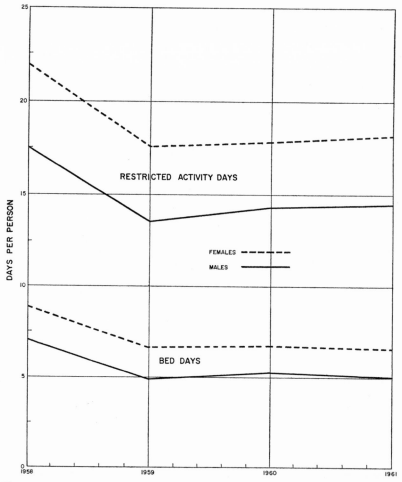

Figure 3. Days of restricted activity and bed disability for males and females, 1958–61. The number of days of restricted activity in 1961 (16.5) was slightly higher than the number in 1959 and 1960 but considerably lower than the 20.0 days for the flu epidemic year of 1958; the number of bed-days also varied, with 5.8 reported in 1961. The source of these data is *Health, Education, and Welfare Trends,* 1962 edition, p. 20.

Table 38. Restricted Activity and Bed Disability for Fiscal Years 1958–61, by Sex and for the Sexes Combined

Age	Both Sexes				Males				Females			
	1958	1959	1960	1961	1958	1959	1960	1961	1958	1959	1960	1961
*Restricted Activity Days Per Person**												
All	20.0	15.8	16.2	16.5	17.7	13.6	14.3	14.6	22.2	17.9	18.0	18.3
0–4	13.2	10.8	10.8	11.3	12.8	11.3	11.0	11.2	13.6	10.3	10.6	11.4
5–14	16.4	12.1	11.6	10.6	16.0	12.1	11.4	10.8	16.8	12.0	11.9	10.5
15–24	13.5	9.3	9.8	10.4	10.8	6.9	7.7	8.6	15.8	11.5	11.6	12.0
25–44	15.8	13.1	13.9	14.4	12.4	8.9	10.6	10.4	19.0	17.0	17.0	18.1
45–64	25.4	20.2	21.6	21.9	22.6	17.4	19.1	20.1	28.0	22.8	23.9	23.6
65+	47.3	38.0	37.8	40.1	45.2	35.9	36.8	38.7	49.1	39.7	38.6	41.2
Bed-Days Per Person†												
All	7.8	5.8	6.0	5.8	6.9	4.9	5.3	5.0	8.7	6.6	6.7	6.6
0–4	5.8	4.6	4.7	4.8	5.2	4.7	4.9	4.8	6.4	4.5	4.6	4.8
5–14	7.8	5.2	5.0	4.4	7.6	5.0	4.7	4.1	8.0	5.3	5.2	4.6
15–24	6.3	3.9	4.1	4.1	4.9	2.9	2.9	3.1	7.6	4.9	5.1	4.9
25–44	5.8	4.9	4.8	4.9	4.4	3.5	3.8	3.4	7.0	6.2	5.8	6.3
45–64	8.8	6.6	7.4	6.8	7.7	5.6	6.7	6.2	9.8	7.5	8.2	7.4
65+	16.3	12.1	13.6	13.8	16.0	10.5	13.1	12.9	16.6	13.5	13.9	14.5

Source: *Health, Education, and Welfare Trends*, 1962 edition, p. 20.

* Day on which usual activities were reduced because of illness or injury.

† Day on which person was in bed more than half the daylight hours because of illness or injury.

The other basic category of data comes from prevalence studies — surveys taken during a given time, such as a day, a month, a quarter; the information they yield tells us how prevalent illness was during that period, how long it lasted for those surveyed, its causes, and so on. I shall not attempt to spell out here the results of various prevalence studies,[10] but several comments can be made.

Illness prevalence surveys have since 1958 resembled unemployment surveys in kind and approach. Unemployment rates are given as, for example, percentages of the civilian labor force. We can calculate illness rates and compare them with those for unemployment. For 1960 the illness rates were 1.7 per cent for bed-days and 4.3 per cent for restricted activity days.[11] Unemployment for 1960 was 5.6. Our estimates for 1910 suggest 7.0 per cent for bed-days, 13.0 for restricted activity days, compared with a 1910 unemployment rate of 5.9. This suggests that illness has become less of an aggregate challenge to economic security than unemployment.

Long-term disability, with its attendant high expenses, is a major problem. In one survey of the disabled in 1950 over a third were found to be incapacitated for longer than a year. In a 1954 survey, 5.3 million people had been disabled for six months or more. Illness varies greatly by age. Table 38 and Figure 3 illustrate this for two categories, and illness varies also according to characteristics other than age. For example, the very young and the aged are sick oftener than the average person, and the illnesses of the aged are much longer, though age is a relatively unimportant factor for persons twenty to fifty. The probability of a long illness increases markedly as a person gets older. Females are more likely to be ill than males, but less likely to be disabled for a long time. Disabling illnesses of all lengths are commoner among nonwhites than whites. Low-income groups suffer more frequent and more serious illnesses than the middle- and upper-income groups, but otherwise in-

[10] For a brief summary, including citations, see Turnbull, Williams, Cheit, *op. cit.*, pp. 296–302.

[11] That is, the number of bedridden was 1.7 per cent of the total population; the number restricted was 4.3 per cent. In the same sense in 1960 unemployment as a percentage of the total labor force was 5.6 per cent. We calculated these percentages by dividing the total population into the totals for bed-days and restricted activity days respectively. Note what this means and what it does not mean: it means that for the survey days in question the given percentages of the population were bedridden or restricting their activity; but it is not an annual summation; it is an average of daily proportions for days in selected months or quarters.

come does not appear to have an important influence. (One might suggest, however, that a cause of low income may be prolonged illness.) Employed people are, on the average, much healthier than the unemployed. Certain occupations are more hazardous than others, and some occupations are associated with undesirable moral and economic characteristics. The effect of rural and urban residence upon the probability of illness is not clear, but the urban group appears to be healthier. Unmarried people are more likely to be sick than married people, especially at older ages. Illness is much commoner in the winter than in the summer, primarily because of the many brief mild respiratory diseases in the winter.[12]

Illness in the Aged [13]

The proportion of aged persons with chronic illness (heart disease, cancer, diabetes, arthritis) is about twice the proportion of persons under 65 with such illness. Though the aged constitute about 9 per cent of the total population, they make up more than 55 per cent of all persons with limitations due to chronic illness. The number of days spent in a general hospital is two to three times as large, on the average, for those 65 and over as for younger people. In the period June 1957–June 1959, the elderly person made 6.8 visits to the doctor compared with 4.8 visits by the rest of the population. This incidence problem is compounded by the diminished income of retirement. To this point we shall return later.

Income and Expense Problems

For the employed, nonoccupational illness should pose the same budgetary and expense problems as occupational illness. Some exceptions might be admitted, because more nonoccupational illness may be of a prolonged kind, implying not only greater loss of income but relatively costlier medical treatment.

For the person not earning wages — housewife or retirant — the problem is different. Income loss is not relevant, medical expenses are; their magnitude depends upon the illness, with the more serious problems (those caused by costlier treatment) likely to be concentrated in such groups as the aged.

[12] See Turnbull, Williams, and Cheit, *op. cit.*, p. 301.
[13] See United States Congress, United States Senate, Special Committee on Aging, Staff Report, *Basic Facts on the Health and Economic Status of Older Americans* (87th Congress, 1st Session), 1961.

The assumption made here is that the wage earner's nondeferrable budget (exclusive of medical expense) is the same (for the short run — six months or less) as it was for the economically unemployed: $4,200 a year for a family of four. (When the discussion turns to presenting income restoration data this budget can be circumvented, thanks to an estimating method applied by Alfred M. Skolnik of the Social Security Administration. But we include the figure here for comparative purposes.) In 1910 I also suggest that a nondeferrable budget would approximate that of the economically unemployed; the figures in that case ranged from $550 to $785.

Average medical expense I hesitate to try to estimate. One set of figures we arrived at were per-capita medical payments, which averaged $10 in 1910, $30 in 1929, and $147 in 1960.[14] Again, however, when I come to examine how economic security programs meet medical expenses, I shall circumvent these specific figures.

The Preventive Ideal and Current Reality

One suggested ideal along the preventive route in nonoccupational illness is this: minimize illness and, when death must come, let it be quick. Whether we shall ever realize this goal is debatable; certainly some current indications are that more people are kept alive than formerly, but only at considerable expense.[15] I believe that in the near future, at least, meeting medical expenses will continue to be a problem of some magnitude for many persons; alleviation therefore again looms importantly upon the scene.

The Alleviative Ideal and Current Reality

Opinions vary as to what might be regarded as an alleviative ideal in restoring lost income and meeting medical expenses. My own prejudices lead me to suggest the following, which is not very different from the indemnity approach under workmen's compensation: (1) Providing,

[14] For 1929 and 1960 I first summed direct payments for health and medical care, health insurance benefits, public expenditures for health (which included construction monies), and philanthropic payments, and then divided this sum by the population. Data from *Social Security Bulletin*, November, 1961, and *Historical Statistics of the United States*, p. 7, 179.

[15] Lest I be misunderstood, I by no means suggest that it is undesirable to seek to prolong life. I merely note that it requires outlays greater than formerly and my concern is with meeting these outlays.

for the short run, sufficient income to meet nondeferrable expense, or approximately two thirds of the wage at the time the nonoccupational illness forced the worker off the job.[16] Whatever the source of income, public or private, realistic maximums should be set so that a flat-benefit system does not result. In the case of workmen's compensation I recommended meeting nondeferrable expenses during the entire period of the disability. Here I propose doing so only during the short run of six months or a year, basically because of policing problems. As a public program, workmen's compensation has various checks which permit abuses to be policed; I am less sanguine about policing abuses under wholly private approaches. (2) Providing, over the long run (after six months or a year), two thirds of the nondeferrable budget. Here, however, the nondeferrable budget increases to the full budget, less taxes (if such substitute income is nontaxable). This implied self-help on the part of the ailing is not to the full two thirds (unless the substitute income is taxed), but rather on the order of 20 per cent. (3) Providing full medical expense, as for a period of a year, and then a program in which, for example, 20 per cent co-insurance is used. Ideally it would be desirable to cover all medical expenses, but the incidence of nonoccupational illness is such that this poses insurance cost problems. (4) Providing some form of idemnity for those permanent disabilities which do not absolutely curtail future earning power but which reduce it. Though there are considerable difficulties in working out a precise, actuarial set of payments, such plans are in operation.

We shall now see how current programs and the programs of 1910 measure up against these suggested standards (Table 39).

The Social Security Administration has, within the past decade, made estimates of short-term (six months or less) income losses due to nonoccupational illness and protection against such income loss.[17] The average number of workdays lost in 1960 because of short-term illness ranged between seven and eight for all classes of employees; the total estimated income loss was $8.6 billion. The principal forms of protection against such loss of income came from the following programs: paid sick leave; publicly operated funds or private plans under compulsory temporary disability statutes (the Railroad Unemployment Insurance

---

[16] With a city worker's budget of $6,200, this would approximate $4,200.

[17] See Alfred M. Skolnik, "Income-Loss Protection against Short-Term Sickness, 1948–60," *Social Security Bulletin*, January, 1962, pp. 3–11.

Act and the state laws in California, New Jersey, New York, and Rhode Island); and private arrangements through insurance companies or self-insured cash sickness programs.[18]

In 1960 such programs restored 27.7 per cent of lost earnings (compared with 16.6 per cent in 1948, the first year for which estimates are available). The degree of restoration varied by type of program: government-paid sick leave provided the highest (73+ per cent) restoration, private programs the lowest (16.5 per cent) restoration, partly because about half of the private wage and salary workers in nondisability states had no protection whatsoever.

Table 39. An Index of Nonoccupational Illness Protection in 1910 and 1960 *

Kind of Income Loss	Ideal	1910	1960
Short-term†	100% of nondeferrable budget (approx. 67% of city worker family budget equivalent)	<5%	28%
Long-term	67% of nondeferrable budget (approx. $5,400)	<5%	28%
Medical expense	80% of total (in effect 20% co-insurance)	<5%	27%

* These are global data and apply to *all* the disabled irrespective of the degree of coverage under public and/or private programs.

† Six months or less.

If we seek to offset not the total income lost but the nondeferrable expenses (two thirds of the "income"), the level of restoration is, obviously, higher. For 1960 it would approximate 40 per cent instead of 28 per cent. If we make a further adjustment and consider only that category of persons who are covered (eligible for income restoration) the percentage of income made up rises to 60 per cent: that is, those people who were covered received 60 per cent of their nondeferrable budgets for a period up to as long as a half year.

In 1910 state temporary disability laws did not exist; paid sick leave, though not unknown, was minimal; and insurance protection was largely if not entirely of the individual variety — that is, not provided on a group basis at the place of work. I estimate that income restoration provided as a matter of right through a formal program was less than 5 per

[18] There is, of course, a sizable amount of informal paid sick leave (often at full pay) provided by small employers, including that for the hired man of the farmer and the domestic servant. I am indebted to Robert J. Meyers for this observation.

cent of a nondeferrable budget. A common form of help in those days was taking up a collection for the injured person.[19]

For want of a better definition I shall define a long term as one lasting more than six months. As suggested earlier, in the long run the nondeferrable budget becomes the full budget. Here, starting again with our $6,200 figure, we deduct $100 for working expenses, leaving $6,100. If the substitute income (the maintained income) is tax-free, we take off $700, leaving $5,400.

The principal source of public protection at present is the disability insurance provided under OASDI. Disability must be total (the victim unable to engage in any substantial gainful activity), and must have lasted six months. Payments under this program began in July, 1957, and the law was amended and liberalized in 1958 and 1960. Various private programs frequently are supportive in long-term disability cases; a disabled person may also receive payments from his pension accumulation.

The estimate made here of income loss from long-term disability in 1962 is in the neighborhood of $7.5 billion. OASDI disability payments were $1.105 billion, other public and private payments were perhaps sufficient to bring this to $2.0 billion, or approximately 28 per cent of income restored. Note that this is about the same as the short-term restoration (27.7 per cent). The OASDI program is much more extensive in its coverage than are the temporary disability laws, but paid sick leave and similar provisions are much more important in the short run, and, in effect, disappear as time goes on. The disability feature of the OASDI program will become increasingly important as time passes; it is likely, in the near future at least, that long-term disability will be better provided for than short-term.

As in our discussion of short-term disability, total income lost can be reduced to the nondeferrable expense level; here the nondeferrable budget is different, however. It is $6,200 less $700 (taxes) and $100 (expenses saved by not working), or $5,400. The degree of income restoration to all the long-term disabled is 31 per cent. If we consider only those persons who are receiving some long-term disability income maintenance, the degree of income restoration to them is about 45 per cent.

[19] For some trenchant comments on then and now, see R. L. Duffus, "The Slave or Welfare State," Ch. IX, in *Nostalgia, U.S.A.*, New York: Norton, 1963.

Total private medical expenditures in 1960 were $19.6 billion; in 1948, $7.6 billion. This averaged $110 per capita in 1960 and $53 in 1948.[20] Hospital care, services of physicians and dentists, and drugs and drug sundries accounted for over 80 per cent of the total; of these expenditures, 26.7 per cent were met by insurance of one kind or another in 1960 and 8.2 per cent in 1948.

In occupational disability we have a public program, workmen's compensation, providing a degree of restoration of lost wages, some help with medical expense, and certain indemnities for permanent disability. To cover income loss resulting from nonoccupational disability, there are also various public programs: the five temporary disability-income statutes, the sick-leave provisions of governments as employers, and the disability provisions of OASDI. But in the medical expense area no basic public program provides protection as a matter of right.[21]

The debate that has gone on over the last decade or two focuses upon two issues: the adequacy of current protection against medical expenses and the role of the government in providing protection. Whether one views current protection as adequate or not depends upon one's criteria. Those who believe that an adequate job is being done or at least that satisfactory progress is being made under the present voluntary approach point to the fact that in 1960, 131.9 million persons (nearly 75 per cent of the population) were covered by hospital expense insurance; 121 million had physician's and surgeon's expense protection; and 27.4 million had major medical insurance.[22] But if one uses more rigorous criteria — looks at those not protected or at the extent of protection for those with some coverage — then he is likely to be more critical. A study by Herman M. and Anne R. Somers concludes: "No more than 8 per cent had any broad protection against medical costs."[23]

[20] Louis S. Reed, "Private Medical Care Expenditures and Voluntary Health Insurance 1948–1960," *Social Security Bulletin*, December, 1961, pp. 3–11.

[21] There are, to be sure, programs extending protection based upon need. These programs, where federal participation is involved, include medical assistance to the aged, initiated in October 1960 under the Social Security Amendments of 1960 (the Kerr-Mills bill, Public Law 86–778); and vendor payments for medical care under the categorical programs for old-age assistance; aid to dependent children, aid to the blind, and aid to the permanently and totally disabled. These payments are not inconsequential; in fiscal 1962 they totaled $713 million; the rate in February, 1964, was over $1 billion a year.

[22] See the annual *Sourcebook of Health Insurance Data*, New York: Health Insurance Institute, 1962.

[23] *Doctors, Patients, and Health Insurance*, Washington: Brookings Institution, 1961, p. 365. This is a fascinating and detailed discussion of the problem and is required reading for anyone interested in these issues.

Two kinds of question can be asked about government's role in the medical expense area, the first abstract — what should the role of government be? — the second concrete — given the temper of the times, what is the role of government likely to be?

Let us look at the second first. One may doubt that the near future, at least, will witness enactment of any medical expense legislation for the general population. Likely proposals will deal with one major problem: medical care for the aged and whether such protection should remain, as in the 1960 Kerr-Mills legislation, on a grant-in-aid basis, or should be incorporated into OASDI. My own prejudices lead me to favor the latter course because it offers protection as a matter of right, and because, since the Social Security Administration is a going organization, it is administratively more efficient to use it rather than setting up another new chain of bureaucracy.[24]

It is unlikely that we shall see a general government medical expense program in the near future, so it is perhaps injudicious to take a position on the issue. Since private efforts have resulted in vastly increased protection and a private system of some consequence is in being, I prefer not to see a general government protection program begun at this time, and to see attention and study devoted instead to the feasibility of providing a government program at the fringe, where it is most needed, and giving protection as a matter of right.[25]

An Evaluation: The Risks, The Programs

Between 1955 and 1960 illness decreased by one half to two thirds in the aggregate.[26] The nature and incidence of illness has changed; it happened less in childhood, more in old age, at which time it requires costlier treatment. With a few exceptions (such as the five temporary disability laws) there are no public programs (explicit income mainte-

[24] Another strong reason might be adduced. For such old-age protection to apply, a state must enact legislation (a plan) approved by the Social Security Administration. By March, 1964, thirty-six jurisdictions — few in the South — had such plans, though five more states had plans scheduled to go into operation in the future. About half the recipients were in three states (California, Massachusetts, New York). The need is clear; the response has not been overwhelming, though it is certainly improving.

[25] Were the protection to be federal with universal coverage I would be less unfavorable. But if it is on a state basis with limited coverage, I am unfavorable. The record of private health insurance — in coverage and in degree of restoration — compares very well with such laws as unemployment insurance and workmen's compensation.

[26] Several critics who have read this section suggest I am too optimistic about the size of the decrease.

nance as a right) in this area of economic insecurity. In place of a floor of public protection we find a vast miscellany of private approaches ranging from paid sick leave through diverse forms of insurance to prepaid medical care. In the extent of coverage and the degree of income maintenance these private approaches are, however, doing as good a job as unemployment insurance or workmen's compensation is. It may be argued that the private approaches do not provide protection where it is most needed, and there is truth in that argument. But there is also truth in the indictment that gaps exist in unemployment insurance and workmen's compensation. The idea of a federal program providing a floor of protection both for lost income and for medical expense has merit. The possibility of such a program's being enacted is very dim, however, though it is true that the 1960 medical care for the aged programs were altered and incorporated into OASDI in 1965.[27]

If public programing were to be a matter of state law I would far prefer to see developments left to private enterprise, whose record, when compared with the states', is not at all unfavorable. Moreover, states are reluctant to compete in improving social welfare standards. Yet whatever one may say about the degree of competition in the private sector of the economy, there is little doubt that a sufficient amount of it exists to permit continuous improvement. On this I rest my case.

[27] For one point of view see Harold B. Meyers, " 'Medicare,' The Cure That Could Cause a Setback," *Fortune*, May, 1963, pp. 131–33, 167–79.

■ SOME SPECIAL ISSUES
AND CONCLUSIONS

IN EVERYTHING thus far we have been talking of averages (defined here as means) of three kinds: (1) average incidence of insecurity, as for example in unemployment or illness; (2) average income loss, or its counterpart average, expense increase, resulting from the insecurity; (3) average ability to meet these insecurities. The use of averages does not necessarily yield a true picture of the kinds of situations we are discussing, for a number of reasons.

Averages may be affected by extremes which cancel each other out and distort the dimensions of a problem. For example, if medical costs average $50 per person, one person might actually have expenses of $50, another $100, and a third $0. Yet the average remains $50, which clearly understates the problem for the person with expenses of $100. Or, if average ability to meet such expenses is $50 with the same extremes as before, the problem may again be understated if the person with $100 cost has $0 ability. If society had an acceptable way of transferring ability to meet expenses to persons who need it, the average would present a truer picture. Though insurance is a device that does this, it is often optional and does not necessarily accomplish the transfer.

Insofar as averages are produced by prevalence studies, another kind of distortion may result. For example, the unemployment rates resulting from the monthly survey tell us how many people in the civilian labor force are unemployed on a survey day. But in themselves the rates do not show how many people have been out of work for six months. This information can be obtained by asking additional questions of the respondent and is available. But it does not show up in the rate. An unemployment rate of 4 per cent would be much less of a problem if it were the result of completely different persons' being unemployed each month than if it meant, as it does, that some people are unemployed month after month.

The Poverty Problem

Averages may thus disguise the extent of a number of problems concerning both the impact of insecurity and people's ability to cope with insecurity. Though these problems are obviously related, the latter is more frequently emphasized than the former; in its broadest reaches it is defined as the problem of poverty.

In its most extreme factual form the poverty problem is this: forty or fifty million Americans — about a fourth of the population — are currently living in poverty.[1] As Dwight Macdonald says: "Not just below the level of comfortable living, but real poverty in the old-fashioned sense of the word — that they are hard put to it to get the mere necessities, beginning with enough to eat."[2] Such poverty is still at the self-help stage — without public or private assistance of any kind given on the basis of need. How close such assistance can bring these people to the level of comfortable living may be questioned; "nobody starves, but every fourth citizen rubs along on a standard of living below minimal."[3] This fourth also includes many of the employed — people employed at substandard wages — as well as numbers of the unemployed, the aged, the sick, and other groups.[4]

In the following discussion we shall ask what the qualitative characteristics of the impoverished are, and also what the characteristics of the people written about in these pages are. Quantitatively, how much of the poverty described above results from the economic insecurities we have been analyzing? What was the pattern of half a century ago?

The impoverished are frequently described, in their internal charac-

[1] See Michael Harrington, *The Other America: Poverty in the United States,* New York: Macmillan, 1962. Also note Gabriel Kolko, *Wealth and Power in America,* New York: Praeger, 1962; and James N. Morgan, Martin H. David, Wilbur J. Cohen, and Harvey E. Brazer, *Income and Welfare in the United States,* New York: McGraw-Hill, 1962.

[2] In his book review; see "Our Invisible Poor" in the *New Yorker,* January 19, 1963, pp. 82–132.

[3] *Ibid.,* p. 132.

[4] The one fourth is not a sacred figure, however. Leon Keyserling suggests, in *Poverty and Deprivation in the U.S. — The Plight of Two-Fifths of a Nation,* Washington, D.C.: Conference on Economic Progress, 1964, that the figure is closer to 40 per cent. Conversely, Herman P. Miller, in an article in the *New York Times Magazine* for April 21, 1963, prefers to define the poor as families in the bottom fifth of the income distribution. Robert J. Lampman, in a study released in August, 1963 (for the Council of Economic Advisers), sets poverty cutoff budget points at $1,250 a year for a single person, $1,750 for a couple, $2,700 for a family of four. He concludes that 34 million Americans are living in genuine poverty.

teristics, as people who cannot help themselves — who are neither psychologically nor intellectually equipped for the task. Externally, they are the aged, the nonwhite, the members of broken families or families without a worker.

The economically insecure we have been analyzing are different, though they overlap with the impoverished. Our economically insecure certainly include some who cannot help themselves, but many are simply the short-run victims of economic circumstances who will, given time, work their way out. Externally our insecure include the aged, the nonwhite, and so on, and also people of many other descriptions.

The differences between the two groups may become clearer if we look at the quantitative impacts of premature death, old age, economic unemployment, and illness upon poverty. These four forces could be regarded as causing poverty, but they are not the only causes. Moreover, the existence of a public and private economic security system means that not all the victims of such insecurities as unemployment and illness become poor.

Quantitatively, premature death, old age, unemployment, and illness appear to play a smaller role today than they did fifty years ago as the causal forces of poverty, for two reasons: first, on balance, these forces of insecurity have lessened; second, and conversely, explicit income maintenance programs have been introduced, most of them nonexistent in 1910.

Some very general estimates about these questions, based on my own estimates from various materials, are shown in the accompanying tabulation. The 1910 figures have implicit in them the fact that a much larger amount of economic security was provided, for example, in the homes of relatives; today security is provided in more explicit forms. For 1960 a $4,000 income level was used as a cutting-off point; for 1910 this budget was carried backward, adjusting for changing price and consumption levels. It is perhaps too obvious to mention that the poor of 1910 did without many more things than the poor of 1960 do.

	Ideal	*1910*	*1960*
Extent of poverty........	0	30–35% of the population (28–30 million people)	20–25% of the population (36–45 million people)
Amount of poverty caused by premature death, old age, economic unemployment, illness	0	>2/3	<1/2

133

Very hesitantly I hazard that the psychological causes of poverty are increasing (though I recognize that the immigrants of the early part of the century had psychological and other difficulties in adjusting to our industrial system) and the economic (premature death, old age, and so on) lessening. If the economic causes decrease then, relatively, other causes increase. But these noneconomic forces have been increasing also in absolute terms as the complexity and the tempo of society have increased.

If this line of reasoning can be upheld, it is clear that the kinds of economic security programs — maintaining income or defraying expense — we have been talking about would be of limited use. Implicitly, we have been thinking of the person willing and able to work unless he is sick, and not of the person psychologically insecure and therefore unable to work. Nor have we looked at substandard conditions as causes of poverty, though certainly they must be of considerable consequence. This leads to the thought that, even if the ideal kinds of income-maintenance programs we have been talking of were realized, the need for other approaches to poverty would still be great.

One may suggest therefore that "hard-core" poverty and economic insecurity (as we have been using the latter term) require two basically different approaches. Insofar as poverty comes from within and insofar as personality traits can be altered, what is required is an extensive program to accomplish this alteration,[5] a program altering the environment people work in, reducing or abolishing discrimination in employment, for example. And, where the alteration cannot be achieved, continuation of social welfare programs is necessary.[6]

Economic insecurity, in our terms, requires a different kind of treatment (though those of our economically insecure who are also intellectually and psychologically incapable of helping themselves are also included in the poor group, of course). On the preventive side, we need additional effort to reduce premature death, to lower involuntary un-

[5] For a supplementary though by no means contradictory approach see Robert F. Kennedy, "What About a Peace Corps Spirit at Home?," *Saturday Review*, May 25, 1963, pp. 20–21.

[6] How many people can be changed is a question to which I have never found a satisfactory answer. Certainly at the surface level a good deal more appears capable of being done, through education, retraining, and allied methods. At a deeper level, one might be less optimistic about, e.g., how much initiative or responsibility can be inculcated. For some stark comments see Julius Horwitz, "The Grim State of Welfare," *Look*, March 26, 1963, pp. 72–80.

employment, to prevent illness.[7] On the alleviative side our concern has been with programs providing benefits as a matter of right. The poverty problem, on the other hand, uses, fundamentally, the need approach.[8] Both, of course, seek to maintain income.

Economic insecurity in the broadest sense results from insufficient income, an insufficiency with internal causes, inability to hold a job, for example, or with external causes, such as accidental injury. Both create an income and expense problem.

The causes of economic insecurity about which we have been talking — premature death, old age, economic unemployment, illness — do indeed contribute to poverty in the sense in which that term is more broadly used. But these causes are only part of those that lie behind poverty: substandard conditions, broken homes, maladjustment (to move from wide to narrow causes) all play a role. As long as we concentrate upon the person who can help himself, the techniques of prevention and alleviation (here including more adequate income maintenance) are applicable. But when other, personal problems are to be dealt with, a different and broader approach is required.[9]

Poverty is a problem broader than the problems discussed in this book. Solving these problems will of course help to reduce poverty, but enough of it will remain so that other and more comprehensive measures will have to be taken.

Economic Insecurity in the Last Half Century

Let us now try to draw together various of the factual threads running through this analysis. In this section we shall deal with insecurity,

[7] An illustration of the difference between the two groups of people we are discussing is to be found in the area of unemployment. If employment levels were raised, we would presumably reach a point where only "hard-core" unemployment remained. Increasing employment (i.e., reducing unemployment) illustrates the kind of preventive approach I have been suggesting. Tackling the problems of the hard-core unemployed exemplifies the education and retraining approach needed to solve the poverty problem.

[8] Some semantic distinctions must be made. Certainly if a person can exhibit "need" he has a "right" to be helped. But here right is used in the sense that the need does not have to be exhibited. For an example of a current program that uses the need approach see the analysis in the *New York Times* for August 28, 1963, of the food stamp program for needy families, a program of the Agriculture Department which simultaneously helps families on welfare and increases the use of the nation's abundant agricultural resources.

[9] Possibly the dependent children problem affords the best example of what cannot be resolved through the kinds of economic security programs we have been analyzing; that problem requires a quite different kind of attack.

135

in the next with economic security programs, and then conclude with appraisal and recommendations.

First we shall look at various quantitative aspects of insecurity. Aggregatively, summing up all the perils, there has been a decrease in the frequency of economic insecurity caused by premature death, old age, economic unemployment, and illness, though as noted below certain of these insecurities are individually greater than they once were. As indicated above (pp. 14–18), mortality rates have decreased during 1910–60 for those under 65, where premature death is a problem. Old age has increased as an economic insecurity problem; for one thing, there are more old people, absolutely and relatively, than there were in 1910, and the jobs for those over 65 are considerably fewer than they were earlier. One major reason, incidentally, why old age has become a greater problem is that premature death has become a lesser one.

Economic unemployment is at about the same level as it was in 1910, though it is much lower than it was in the 1930's; one important fact is that we are unlikely to witness anything like the joblessness of that decade, so this presentation accepts the idea that there has been a decrease in unemployment insecurity during 1910–60, even though the rates may be the same. Illness, occupational as well as nonoccupational, is relatively less frequent than it was a half century ago, whether one measures it in bed-days or in industrial deaths.

One may conclude that the decrease in insecurity from premature death and illness has more than offset the increase in insecurity resulting from old age. The insecurity of unemployment has remained about at the same level from 1910 to 1960, though 1960 was generally better than any year from 1911 to 1941, a few years in the 1920's excepted.

In essence this improvement, this lessening of the frequency of insecurity, has been a result of the effectiveness of the preventive approach. Society — in both private and public ways — has employed a variety of measures that have worked: improvement in the work environment with a consequent reduction in employee (and hence premature) deaths; monetary and fiscal policies which have prevented a repetition of the unemployment witnessed in the 1930's; the development of antitoxins and the reduction of contagious diseases.

One may conjecture that further improvement will take place in the future. Earlier mortality projections on page 18 provide quantitative indications for premature death. I foresee a major breakthrough in cures for degenerative diseases, which will lower morbidity rates. One may also contend that the preventive route will, in the long run, reduce unemployment below the 6 per cent level of the early 1960's.

This leaves old age. Here the problem will increase in two ways as the number of the aged increases both absolutely and relatively and the opportunities for employment after 65 do not. Quantitatively the reduction of insecurity in premature death, illness, and unemployment will more than offset the increase in insecurity from old age; on net balance this will be a less insecure world tomorrow than it is today, just as today it is less insecure than it was yesterday. I leave it to the reader to speculate whether insecurity in the larger sense — by whatever criteria one wishes to apply — will increase or decrease.

Economic Security Programs in the Last Half Century

The most obvious characteristics of the pattern emerging over the last fifty years are two. First is the development of a formal and explicit income maintenance system which has replaced an informal "service-in-kind" approach. Second has been government programs providing a basic layer of income maintenance protection in all but the nonoccupational illness category, though even in that category partial programs exist. Thus, the first line of protection today is not provided by relatives, friends, and charities, but by OASDI, unemployment insurance, workmen's compensation. To this floor of protection there have been added — and they are increasingly being added — income coverings of various depths provided by group and individual insurance and group and individual savings programs of various kinds. Moreover, and this is highly important, income provided by the public programs is offered as a matter of right and not on the basis of need. This was not true in 1910.

We shall shortly begin to evaluate our economic security programs and in the process provide summary detail about each of them. Here, however, a few summarizing comments may be made. The question is this: if the insecurities caused by premature death, old age, unemployment, and illness lead to an income loss and an expense increase of x billion dollars, how much of this is recovered through the various public and private income maintenance programs (excluding such "need" programs as "relief" or "assistance")?

If we use a nondeferrable budget approach, we can make the following global estimates. For those who are covered by public programs, the income maintenance provided by both public and private programs, plus their own resources, meets 60 per cent of the need. The total economic security system is reasonably effective for short-term insecurity. But it breaks down markedly in prolonged insecurity: long unemployment, serious illness, and such frequent occurrences as sickness among the aged.[10] Fifty years ago, with no public right programs, explicit income maintenance was at 20 to 30 per cent. The figure was this high largely because so many of the aged were working. Over a half century, then, we have more than doubled our income maintenance effectiveness, though we still fall short of our ideal by some 30 to 40 per cent.

For those not covered by public programs and thus without a publicly provided floor of protection, income restoration is much less, perhaps on the order of 30 per cent. Those not covered by public programs are unfortunately also less likely to be covered by such private programs as are provided at the place of employment — group plans, for example. That is, an agricultural laborer or domestic servant not covered by workmen's compensation or unemployment insurance is also unlikely to have an employer who provides group insurance. Fifty years ago the income maintenance level might have approximated 20 per cent for this group. Maintenance would have been less than that available fifty years ago to those currently covered by public programs, since the currently covered tend to be today — and were fifty years ago — in the higher paying occupations; they can and could afford proportionately more insurance and other forms of protection.

If we gloss over the complexities caused by the fact that no over-all public program exists for illness, we can pull our guesses together as follows.

At present about 60 per cent of the population is covered (directly or through the primary breadwinner) by public programs in premature death, old age, unemployment, and illness. And of the income losses (or expense increases) incurred by this group, public programs and private supplements restore 60 per cent. If we except the prolonged cases, the degree of income restoration rises appreciably. Fifty years ago this 60

[10] If one uses customary expenditures rather than the budget, income restoration is less for higher income groups primarily because public programs have benefit ceilings and private programs may also have certain limits, such as maximum surgical payments allowable.

138

per cent of the population would have had no coverage under public programs, and income maintenance for them would have been about 30 per cent, brought up to this level by the relatively numerous employment opportunities available for older persons.

Currently 30 to 40 per cent of the population is not, in the aggregate, covered by public programs in the four fields of economic insecurity under discussion, though for premature death and old age OASDI coverage is nearly universal. Income restoration for this group is markedly less, possibly 30 per cent, although this may be high. Fifty years ago their income restoration was 20 per cent or less. This group probably contributes more than proportionately to the poor class mentioned earlier in this chapter.

The opening chapter promised that economy security programing would be measured first by general criteria and then with some special yardsticks. We now turn to the first of these tasks, using the standards of freedom, justice, economic progress, and economic stability developed by Kenneth E. Boulding.[11]

Economic freedom will be interpreted in terms of area of choice. The wider the area of choice open to a person, the greater his economic freedom. And, presumably, taking into account the rights of others, I would agree that the wider his choice the more desirable a person's situation. There can be little doubt that insecurity limits economic freedom: income is curtailed and along with it the consumer's choice. Or medical expenses increase and income must be allocated to meet them, again restricting choice.

Of the economic security programs, two kinds must be distinguished: programs that are compulsory in their application and those that are voluntary. The latter are easier to dispose of. If a program is voluntary — the individual purchase of life insurance, for example — economic freedom is not altered at the purchase stage: a person is free to buy or not to buy. But his future freedom may be affected by the decision made now; failure to buy now may result in a later loss of freedom, as in the event of premature death. But in the larger sense individual freedom is not limited, though an unwise choice may later restrict it. Compulsory programs pose a different problem: the compulsion may come from two sources. First, under public programs such as OASDI, the force of

[11] See his *Principles of Economic Policy*, Englewood Cliffs, N.J.: Prentice-Hall, 1958, Chs. 1–5, 10.

law compels acceptance; a person is not free to decide whether he will or will not be covered by the program.[12] Second, in private programs such as group insurances provided at the place of employment, choice is also restricted; often all new employees must join.[13]

All this suggests that free choice is restricted by these plans before the insecurity happens; that is, a person has no choice or only limited choice as to whether he will or will not choose to be covered under a program. But, and this is critical, freedom of choice is increased *after* the insecurity because income is maintained at levels it might not otherwise remain at and the area of choice is therefore probably greater than it might otherwise be.

Which is greater, the loss of freedom before or the increase in freedom after the insecurity? I eschew such moral arguments as "compulsory programs are good for people who might otherwise behave imprudently," and instead use an economic line of reasoning following the compensation principle: the marginal utility of the small increments of income paid by the employee in the form of taxes or premiums is *less* than the marginal utility of the larger increments of income received in the form of benefits by the individual after the fact of the insecurity.[14] In this quantified sense, economic freedom is not diminished.

One may conclude, therefore, that our economic security system has not debased economic freedom. Moreover, as Boulding notes, "The 'freedom' that social security gives to the aged and dependent, small as it is, should help rather than hinder the development of that psychological support without which economic support is little more than the perpetuation of misery." [15]

Justice is regarded here in its simplest form, as a kind of relation be-

[12] There are some technical and mostly minor exceptions. From the point of view of the individual employee, clergymen, for but one example, have had certain options about coverage under OASDI. From the point of view of employers, in those states where workmen's compensation is elective or voluntary, choice may be exercised (though certain legal rights may be altered in the process).

[13] Again there are some minor exceptions or distinctions. In many of the programs introduced through collective bargaining the work force at the time could exercise collective freedom of choice to accept or reject the plan. Once accepted, the program restricted the choice of future employees. In some plans escape clauses are to be found; current or future employees may have certain options about joining or not joining.

[14] The principle is, however, much more complex in its application if the payments come from one person and benefits go to another. Interpersonal comparisons with all their attendant complications come into such a situation.

[15] Boulding, *op. cit.*, p. 248.

tween what one contributes to society and what one receives from it. I suggest also that economic insecurity is often unjust in choosing its victim and that economic security programs are a means of trying to remedy this. That is, economic security is a means of providing for those who have served society but who, through no fault of their own, may not have been able to provide for their own security.[16]

Economic progress consists of increase in the national product — of growth in output. As we have seen throughout this book, man may not live by bread alone, but, judging from the income maintenance deficiencies exhibited in our analysis, more bread is one of his pressing needs.

We may get at the impacts of insecurity and security upon economic progress in two ways; first by looking at individuals and initiative, and, second, by inquiring into the larger issue of finances and factories.

Some argue that the economically insecure person is more highly motivated, for he wants to work out of his insecurity. It follows from this theory that the way to increase progress is to keep people insecure. Others argue that the insecure person is submerged and loses whatever drive he had (this presumably is what happens to people in the "culture of poverty"). Some contend that economic security programs reduce initiative and hinder progress, others that a base of security makes people more willing to take risks and therefore facilitates progress. Where does the truth lie? After a search of a decade's literature I believe no one can say. One may suggest that in the aggregate the effect of security and insecurity upon economic progress has been neutral, though certainly visible reactions are evident in some programs and with some people.[17]

The financial implications of economic security programs for progress are quite different. If receipts (from taxes and premiums) exceed disbursements (benefits), reserves are built up through this medium of forced and voluntary saving. If these reserves are invested in real capi-

---

[16] We do not deal here with what some have called the default thesis — that those who have not served society well, who have defaulted on their obligations, require different treatment. I regard this as part of the problem of those who are not able to help themselves. For a much more sophisticated discussion of the whole topic see Richard B. Brandt, ed., *Social Justice*, New York: Prentice-Hall, Inc., 1962. Boulding has a more detailed essay in the same volume, and William K. Frankena's is also valuable.

[17] For a useful summary, see Roberta Nelson's 1957 unpublished Plan B paper for the M.A. degree at the University of Minnesota, "Some Reflections on Security and Incentive." The studies by Oscar Lewis are particularly insightful concerning the culture of poverty; see particularly his *Five Families*, New York: Basic Books, 1959.

tal, future output is greater than it would otherwise be. The questions then are those of fact: have reserves increased, and have they been invested so as to yield increased future output? The answer to the first is yes: reserves in both public and private program accounts have risen year after year, with some deviations, as in OASDI or UC accounts. The answer to the second has two parts: There is little doubt that an important part of the reserves of private program agencies has gone into real capital and that future output has therefore been augmented. It is less easy to say that government reserve accumulations have been or can be used in the same manner. But even if their impact is discounted, the net result has been to make more investable funds available and thus to increase future output over what it would have been.[18]

Economic stability requires answers to two questions: we must know what it is we are trying to keep stable and what we mean by stable. Economic stability is stability of the level of economic activity — that is, of income and employment. Stability itself is the minimization of deviations around a trend line, in this case a growth trend. We should all like to see a steady growth trend with deviations of income and employment around this trend minimized.

Stability does not mean rigidity. It allows for individual variations as long as the aggregates conform. It permits rising prices, though there is no unanimity about the degree of rising prices that is conformable with stability. Insecurity does not square with stability; stability presupposes that incomes are maintained, whereas insecurity implies that they are not.

Economic security programs probably have a mixed effect upon stability, some factors heightening, some lessening, with a net result of partial cancellation. The effects can be looked at in two ways. First are the consequences of tax and premium collections and the offsetting benefits. One can work out a variety of different situations depending upon the assumptions employed: for example, if benefits equal payments in, the net impact should be neutral, provided the consumption and savings patterns of contributors and beneficiaries are equal. If payments in exceed benefits, and the economy is already on the brink of de-

---

[18] The accumulation process can cut the other way. If there is no demand for investable funds, not only do you sacrifice additional future output, but you also suffer from the pressures of deflation. Such idle accumulations are hoards which might just as well be buried in the ground.

flation, the problems may be heightened.[19] Or if the economy is in an inflationary period and payments in exceed benefits, a desirable brake may be imposed upon the upward movement.

Second, different programs operate in different ways as regards stability. Illness is not cyclical, and since reserve accumulations (other than for contingencies) are not common in economic security programs covering illness, the programs tend to be neutral. Unemployment insurance systems, public or private, ideally should be counter-cyclical and should thereby contribute to stability: that is, the systems should increase accumulations in good times and disburse them in bad. The experience rating feature of such programs tends, however, to weaken the counter-cyclical benefits, though on balance there is little doubt but that they contribute to stability. Programs for premature death and old age include reserve accumulations on other than a contingency basis, and they may have economic consequences of the kinds described above. But public programs may also have other impacts. If, for example, OASDI benefits are increased by law in a period of rising prices, instability may be compounded. I suspect that though particular instances of instability can be shown to have arisen from economic security programs, they are minor compared with the impact of monetary and fiscal policies in the broader sense.

Moreover, if we believe that a basic problem of the economy is that it operates at less than full capacity — that there is some tendency for it to drift downward — then perhaps economic security programing increasingly provides a stabilizing check. In 1912–13 economic security benefits, both public and private, from organized income maintenance and health programs (but excluding education), amounted to some $1.2 billion, or 3 per cent of the gross national product.[20] In 1960–61 the figure was $65 billion, or 13 per cent of the gross national product. As Ida Merriam notes: "An established social security system is a stabilizing factor in the economy because of the assured income provided to large segments of the nonworking population, the compensatory expansion of aggregate benefits when employment falls off, the probably wider effect on consumer spending of the knowledge that unemployment benefits will

[19] Indeed, Boulding suggests the recession of 1938 was partly a consequence of the imposition of social security taxes a year earlier.

[20] My estimates made from Ida C. Merriam, "Social Welfare Expenditures, 1960–1961," *Social Security Bulletin,* November, 1962, pp. 3–13.

be available, and the institutional mechanism the system provides for any desired emergency measures." [21]

This section concludes by noting that, in my judgment, the impacts of economic insecurity are negative; though a weak case can be made for uncertainty as an incentive or spur, I believe that insecurity is destructive economically and psychologically. Economic security programs have been positive in their effects. They come off well when evaluated by the criteria of freedom, justice, progress, and stability. This is not to suggest that they are ideal, and it is to a more detailed critical evaluation that we now turn.

Operational Criteria for Evaluating Economic Security Programs

We now proceed to examine economic insecurity and security issues not in broad, abstract terms, but from a more limited, operational point of view. This narrower scope does not, however, lessen the problem of evaluation; if anything this evaluation will require greater detail.

It is difficult if not impossible to appraise preventive approaches, largely because guidelines are absent. Who can say whether we should have expected a malignant disease preventive by now? Or that the toll on the highways is greater than we should realistically expect? I suggest that though we know we ought not to let up in our preventive efforts, except for reduction to zero we have no realistic optimum, and do not know where we ought expect to be. As will shortly be seen, however, it is easier to set up criteria for evaluating alleviative programs.

Evaluation of public and private alleviative programs requires a somewhat different approach. We can appraise both public and private programs in terms of their response (or accommodation) to new perils, their efficiency, and their administration. But private programs involve contractually agreed upon relations between insurer and insured, and one cannot comment, for example, upon such programs' failure to adjust benefits in the same way that one can comment on legislative responsibility in public programs.

There appear to be several marked similarities as well as several marked differences in the evolution of public as against private accommodation to economic insecurity. The challenge of a problem is common to both, and a response is common to both, though the response

---

[21] "Social Security Programs and Economic Stability" in *Policies to Combat Depression*, Princeton: Princeton University Press, 1956, p. 233.

varies: in the public case it may result in a statute, in the private a new form such as the variable annuity. Here the similarity tends to diminish. A private program may be criticized on the score of efficiency, ethics, or economics. But the public program (though this is not true of OASDI) will be criticized more broadly as a general disenchantment develops. This appears to have happened with workmen's compensation — a feeling that, in the past fifty years, it has not lived up to its promises. The same is true, in lesser degree, of the criticisms of unemployment insurance.

Before we turn to a more detailed consideration of individual economic security programs, some general conclusions will be set forth.

From a positive point of view there is little doubt of the advances that have been made in the last half century in accommodation to the hazards of economic insecurity, whether we look at the nature of the response (explicit income as against service programs, for example) or at the level of the response (the amount of income maintenance provided, for example).

But negatively three criticisms can be made. First, both public and private programs respond too slowly to change. One may ask if the variable annuity, ingenious as it was, was not too long in coming. Or one may suggest that we still have no satisfactory public or private economic security accommodation to the problems of economic change — locational, structural, or other.

Second, and this also applies to both public and private programs, there is a tendency to inadequacy. In private programs this may be a matter of income inadequacy or consumers' irrationality or both. In public programs legislatures often fail to face up to the issues.

Third, and this applies primarily to public programs, is the problem of inflexibility, particularly where state programs and state legislative actions are concerned: an adjustment in benefits is desirable, but a legislature hesitates to act for fear industries will leave the state as a result. There is no automatic way in which adjustment can be effected.[22]

Let us now examine the relevant issues in greater detail. What characteristics of today's insecurity appear different from those of earlier years? Three, I believe, are of consequence.

[22] In one midwestern state, for example, legislative deadlocks for six years prevented any change in the unemployment insurance law though such change was desirable from the point of view of both finances and benefits.

145

The first is the problem of economic change. It is my conviction that the tempo of change has increased and its dimensions grown wider. A man in 1960 may have had no greater chance of unemployment than he did in 1910, but I believe that one who did lose his job in 1960 had a harder time getting back into his old line of work than did his counterpart of 1910. Moreover, the unemployed man in 1960 had more trouble, I believe, finding work in his own community than did a person similarly situated in 1910. This adds up to much greater problems of occupational and spatial mobility in 1960 than in 1910. Unemployment insurance is apparently not the optimal solution to such problems as these, and it is only since 1960 that we have started to apply such techniques as area redevelopment and retraining.

The second is the problem of illness. If it is true that fifty years ago one died from disease x in three days whereas today one recovers — but only after expensive hospitalization — then economic security programing ought to be developed in the area of illness. At present we have no governmental floor of protection, though there is a vast range of activity from care of veterans to grants in aid for the aged.

The third is the problem of changing price levels. It ought to be possible in public programs to have flexibility in adjustment to changing prices (as in benefits) without the kind of legislative agony that now often accompanies such changes. Below we shall look into specific suggestions made about this issue; certainly the variable annuity provides one useful approach.

It is my conviction that income maintenance should be provided as a matter of right rather than on the basis of need,[23] for two reasons. First, the economic: right presupposes (at least in the United States) some kind of systematic program permitting a planned relation between costs and benefits. Second, the ethical: right assumes that the beneficiary has directly contributed to the program in one way or another.[24]

Most present American economic security programs extend benefits as a matter of right, much in contrast to the situation fifty years ago.

[23] Again there are semantic entanglements: a person should not have the right to collect unemployment benefits unless he needs them, i.e., is unemployed. But once unemployed, he should be able to collect benefits as a matter of right, without undergoing a means test.

[24] It is for this reason that a good case can be made for contributory systems. Even though something can be said for the lower costs (because of less expensive collection and record-keeping) of a noncontributory system, the noneconomic values are worth the extra cost of the contributory system.

146

Private and social insurances — the bulk of protective programs — fall into this category, and they are increasingly outstripping such need programs as old-age assistance.

Interestingly and perhaps tragically enough it is the poverty class to which the need approach is most commonly applied. In part this may reflect their lack of coverage by other programs, or their having exhausted benefits under them. But it may also be a consequence of the fact that the problems of the poor are less responsive to other approaches: for example, it is difficult to see how aid to dependent children could be built into the same kind of insurance program as exists for premature death.[25]

One must admit, however, that some facets of the benefits-as-rights belief are troublesome. If a man has been frugal, has invested wisely, and has independent means in his old age, I see no reason why he should not nevertheless collect OASDI benefits if he is eligible (as he can do at present). Parallel reasoning would apply to various other examples. But we soon come to borderline (in my judgment) cases where my argument becomes inconsistent: I cannot, for example, so readily accept the idea of a seasonal worker with high earnings collecting unemployment insurance in the off season. Nor can I as easily believe that the part-time worker, the secondary wage earner, and the juvenile unemployed should necessarily collect as a matter of right.[26] On balance, however, the principle of right rather than need is an excellent step in the proper direction.

Income Versus Service

Most economic security programs today are of the income variety. The exceptions are programs in which it appears desirable, for many reasons including control of expenditure, to provide the service directly.[27] Fifty years ago the service approach was the more common, but this was in the context of a situation where most security was pro-

---

[25] Of course insurance or any other kind of program benefits might be extended as a matter of right. This gets us again into the kind of semantic problem of need and right we discussed in the opening chapter.

[26] I am not sure why I have this ambivalent view. Probably it comes from advisory council experience with the unemployment insurance laws and from concern about problems of abuse and misuse.

[27] There are other variations which do not, however, negate this statement. For example, in hospital and medical programs, the recipient of the service may not handle any monetary indemnity; it passes directly from insurer to service vendor. Yet freedom of choice (to select doctor or hospital) is not abridged.

vided implicitly by relatives, friends, and charities. Today the reverse tends to be true: today the security is explicitly provided in the form of money or other income.

This trend is laudable. Moreover, I believe that the present division of income and service programs is generally satisfactory. Unlike other areas where criticism might be sharp, no major suggestions are made here for altering the existing situation. Income payment systems maximize freedom of choice; this is good. But certain kinds of function, such as those undertaken by welfare agencies, may best be provided on a service basis, and should be so provided.[28]

Coverage under public economic security programs should be extended, both because of the economics of income maintenance and because of the ethics of uniform protection. OASDI is close to an optimal position in this respect, but both unemployment insurance and workmen's compensation could be extended.[29]

Because private programs are voluntary, evaluating them is harder. At the risk of mouthing platitudes further exploration and experiment should be encouraged with both conventional insurances and the less conventional supplemental benefits; encourage the extension of coverage by these plans wherever possible; and suggest that they are not substitutes for the floor of public protection.

Possibly the most serious indictment that can be brought against current programs is their inadequacy in restoring income. One reason for this is an original failure to allocate more resources to this problem; another is that benefits once considered adequate have been eroded for various reasons. This latter reason, in turn, reflects the inflexibility of benefit adjustment.

What is adequate is, to be sure, debatable. In a real sense the definition hinges upon what society believes it can afford at its current and prospective income levels, upon the degree of its obligation toward the insecure, and upon the other uses it has for its money. My view of adequacy rests upon the criterion of a minimum nondeferrable expense

[28] For example, child care, as in babysitting for working mothers, may be undertaken much more satisfactorily on a group basis than by the individual income route.

[29] For details about possible extensions see United States Congress, United States Senate, Special Committee on Unemployment Problems, *Report of the Special Committee on Unemployment Problems* (86th Congress, 2nd Session, Report No. 1206), 1960, pp. 88–94; and *State Workmen's Compensation Laws: A Comparison of Major Provisions*, United States Department of Labor, Bureau of Labor Standards, 1962.

budget in the case of income maintenance and upon an added-expense budget where medical care is the problem.

Inadequacy appears to have been greater in 1910 than in 1960, but one may suggest that programs could have been more adequate in 1960. The modern inadequacy has several causes. OASDI is a federal program, and it is easier for a single legislative body to act upon a matter and affect the economy uniformly than it is for more than fifty legislatures to amend laws in ways they believe will put them at a competitive disadvantage.

The specific way in which benefit inadequacy enters public programs is through benefit maximums: state laws may set income benefits at levels which approximate two thirds of the daily wage at the time of injury. But if such a maximum as $45 a week is imposed, and then the average wage in the state rises to $90 a week, you have a flat-rate system that actually restores much less than two thirds of the income. This kind of benefit system is a queer combination of flexibility and rigidity. It is flexible as to the percentage of recovery. Were wages to remain stationary, there would be little problem (even with a flat maximum), provided the maximum were realistically set. But wages have been rising over the decades. The legislatures set the maximums, and they must act to alter the laws — and the legislatures, for various reasons, move most slowly here.

An easy way out of this quandary, one that does not require the legislature to abdicate and that a number of states are using is this: a flexible recovery rate is set, at perhaps 50 per cent of the wage; in addition a flexible maximum is set, such as 60 per cent of the average weekly wage in covered employment. This doubly flexible rate system permits the achievement of both purposes and yet, because the legislature sets the rates, does not require them to relinquish their control.

Inadequacy in private programs is less easily dealt with because there is no taxing authority able to raise the sums required for maintenance and expense. In collectively bargained programs, the problem is choosing between here-and-now direct wage increases on the one hand and deferred fringe benefits on the other. It is possibly a little surprising, in fact, that as much has gone into fringe benefits as has.

Two kinds of problem exist in the area of income security and incentives: people who prefer security program benefits to work, and cases where the existence of a security program causes more intensive use of

149

various facilities than the situation dictates — as when hospital insurance encourages overuse of hospital services — you paid your premium; why not take advantage of the services?

In the first case there certainly are abuses. But my personal judgment is that they are no greater here than in other walks of life, and certainly not of a magnitude to undermine the system. The major correctives are well understood and readily available: clear rules of the game and full communication with the recipients; effective policing (administration) of the program; prompt and equitable punishment for violators.[30]

The problem of overuse or misuse is much harder to handle. Scandal-sheet examples are easy to find: parents use the hospital to babysit their children (or their own parents) over the weekend. I seriously doubt, however, that many do this. Subtler misuse happens where the definition of necessary may be less clear. A cautious and careful physician must decide whether a particular person should go to a hospital or not. At the risk of sounding fatalistic, one can hold the conviction that this is a price society must pay for programs of this kind.

What economic security programs do to costs and prices is a complex matter. We have touched upon the general problem in discussing economic stability. A narrower problem is whether specific programs, such as prepaid medical care, raise medical costs.[31] And a still narrower issue is whether abuse (as in unemployment insurance) or misuse (as in health insurance) raises costs. I suspect they do. Are the increases unreasonable, however that be defined? In unemployment I doubt it; in health insurance perhaps, though again this may be a price that must be paid for such programing.

Pure efficiency might dictate some kind of unified, monolithic, economic security system. But at the cost of that efficiency a pluralistic system is to be preferred. True, this sort of system has gaps and overlaps, creates inequities, and increases bureaucracies. But pluralism, with its emphasis on varied groups, has virtues all its own that outweigh pure

[30] This kind of incentive problem is narrower than the more general issues of security and incentive we have been concerned with in these pages.

[31] Joseph Garbarino, in a carefully reasoned analysis, concludes that health insurance has been a factor in price increases, but the major cause has been the pressure on an inelastic supply of services of a growing demand for more medical care. See his "Price Behavior and Productivity in the Medical Market," *Industrial and Labor Relations Review*, October, 1959, pp. 12–13.

considerations of cost.[32] The American economic security system has developed in this pluralistic direction and I have no criticism to make of that direction of development.[33]

A Balance Sheet

Quantitatively and aggregatively, the threat of insecurity from premature death and illness has lessened in the last half century; has remained about the same for unemployment for 1910 and 1960, though it was at both times vastly less than in the 1930's; and has increased for old age. On balance, insecurity is less.

The faces or characteristics of insecurity have changed. The probability of unemployment may have been no higher in 1960 than in 1910, but re-employment in 1960 called for greater occupational and locational readjustment than in 1910. In illness, the diseases of childhood have given place, as a threat, to the degeneration of old age.

Much of the reduction in insecurity has been the result of consciously directed preventive programs, those directed toward safety (and against premature death), toward sound monetary and fiscal policy (and against unemployment), and toward personal health (and against illness). Prevention can never be fully effective, and we may wonder in such fields as highway safety why it is not more effective. But it may also be that highway deaths would be much greater than they are except for current preventive programs.

Considerable progress has been achieved in a half century in alleviative economic security programing, with the following major improvements: the development of explicit income-maintenance programs in place of implicit, often informal service approaches; income maintenance as a matter of right rather than of need; rises in the level of income maintenance; recognition of the government's role in providing a floor of protection and of the utility of social insurance in this connection; an increasingly important role played by private groups, including insurance carriers, in providing more economical forms of protection (as through group techniques) and programs such as the variable annuity designed to meet new risks.

[32] An excellent statement on this matter is by Clark Kerr, "What Becomes of the Independent Spirit," *Fortune*, July, 1953, pp. 110–11, 134–36.

[33] Though possibly there is some cause for concern. See Ch. 18, "Some Concluding Observations," in Turnbull, Williams, and Cheit, *op. cit.*

But the balance sheet also shows entries on the other side. We are not adjusting to changing risks as rapidly or as well as we should. In the area of illness we have not reached a satisfactory accommodation to the problem, and in unemployment we have not really grappled with the problem of adjustment to change. In some programs, levels of adequacy could be raised. The national income permits such improvement and, at least in some public programs, legislative diffidence is to blame for lack of improvement. Similarly, more flexibility in adjusting to change is desirable, in program coverage, benefit levels, costs, and financing. There appears to be some tendency toward bureaucratic erosion in both public and private economic security programs. To cite but one example: it is more and more often argued that workmen's compensation has not lived up to its promises. How to avoid such erosion is not easy to discern, but many consider it a real problem.

The major persistent economic security problem area is poverty. The kinds of insecurity we have discussed in this book are those capable of solution if people are given the opportunity — problems of occasional income maintenance. Economic security programs are designed to provide this income while a person adjusts to the new situation.

But the problem is those who are "incapable" of helping themselves. As an economist, not a social welfare specialist, I know not the answer, but judging from the current literature, the substance and fact of poverty is our main economic insecurity problem. Insofar as it is psychological in origin it does not yield to the kinds of programs we have discussed here.

I close with a quotation from Frederick Lewis Allen's *The Big Change* (New York: Bantam Books, 1961, p. 257): "We have not stood still . . . the story of our changes is a triumphant one . . . yet we would do well to think of our accomplishment thus far as but the preface to what we may accomplish in the next half-century."

Index

■ INDEX

155